The Marvelous Hand of GOD

Accessing Heaven's Favor Through
Obedience To The Holy Spirit

DR LAWRENCE CHESTER

Copyright © 2019 Dr Lawrence Chester.

Parchment Global Publishing
4152 Barnett St., Philadelphia, PA 19135
www.parchmentglobalpublishing.com

ISBN: 978-1-957009-05-6 (sc)
ISBN: 978-1-957009-06-3 (e)

Library of Congress Control Number: 2021922457

All rights reserved. No part of this book may be reproduced, stored, or transmitted by any means—whether auditory, graphic, mechanical, or electronic—without written permission of both publisher and author, except in the case of brief excerpts used in critical articles and reviews. Unauthorized reproduction of any part of this work is illegal and is punishable by law.

CONTENTS

Acknowledgement ix

Preface xi

Dedication xiii

Introduction xv

Part 1   Naomi's Disappointment Was Ruth's Development: Ruth 1:1-18.

Chapter 1   Decision Time 3

Chapter 2   The Disappointment of Naomi 5

Chapter 3   The Diversion Of Orpah 9

Chapter 4   The Determination of Ruth 12

Part 2   Ruth Engaged In Her Destiny: Ruth 1:19 - 2:1-22.

Chapter 5   Ruth Pursued Her Destiny 16

Chapter 6   Ruth Pressed Into The Presence Of Her Redeemer 20

Chapter 7   Ruth Was Protected By Her Redeemer 23

Chapter 8   Ruth Was Provided For By Her Redeemer 26

Part 3   Ruth Entrusted Herself Fully Under Boaz: Ruth 2:13-23.

Chapter 9   Ruth Encountered Peace 33

Chapter 10   Ruth Was Enriched With Companionship 35

Chapter 11   Ruth Endeavored To Be Blessed And Stayed Blessed....39

Part 4   Ruth's Preparation Produced Greatness: Ruth 3:2-4.

Chapter 12   Ruth Was Obedient To The Spirit's Call.....................47

Chapter 13   Ruth Was Operational To The Spirit's Counsel 52

Chapter 14   Ruth Was Overwhelmed By The Spirit's Comfort 59

Part 5   Ruth Extended Her Legacy: Ruth 3:18 – 4:22.

Chapter 15   Ruth Exercised Patience 67

Chapter 16   Boaz Executed The Power Of Attorney.......................74

Chapter 17   Ruth Enjoys The Promotion 80

Chapter 18   Ruth Embodied The Promise Of The Redeemer 85

Conclusion 89

"Pastor Chester goes deep into the text of the book and brings out the inner pearls of its meaning from a practical standpoint that can speak to many, who have had their lives shaken by issues similar to the 'Ruth experience'. I highly recommend this book to all who are seeking an understanding of why we go through such hard times that 'tries the core of our soul', but yet we survive! **It's mysterious to some and miraculous to others.** Simply put its **'The Marvelous Hand of God'** working upon our lives!"

- Joseph Persaud, President of The Philia Foundation,
Masters in International Economic Affairs,
Masters in Sustainability/Renewable Energy Management

"We are living in the greatest time ever in human history: the culmination of God's redemptive plan for mankind and the consummation of His Kingdom on earth. Lawrence Chester helps us take an important step toward understanding the marvelous hand of God in the ultimate salvation of His people and the restoration of families. 'The Marvelous Hand of God' is a compelling story that grips you from the very first chapter."

- Apostle Dr. Dexter C. Burke,
Walk In the Light Church Of God, Inc

"This is a stirring book written about how a family was able to journey from disaster into the Divine Destiny of God. It is a powerful testimony that reminds us that it's never over until God says it is. This book by my dear friend and colleague, Rev. Lawrence Chester, will warm your heart, stir your faith, motivate your spirit and challenge you to turn over the reins of your life into The Marvelous Hand of God. IT IS A MUST READ."

- Rev. Dr. Aubrey H. Greenidge, M.Th..,
Th.D Christian Holiness Ministries, Inc Director of Risk,
Compliance & Security Nassau Inter-County Express

"A detailed devotional study of the book of Ruth that is designed to propel you into your destiny. "The Marvelous Hand of God" traces the factors which worked in Ruth's life and can work in the life of any believer to take them from the lowest levels of despair to the highest levels of victory."

- Rev Paul R. Watson, Pastor and Author

ACKNOWLEDGEMENT

Above all, I want to acknowledge the direction of the Holy Spirit. Next, I want to give special thanks to my wife, Leila, who spent tireless hours editing the manuscript. Also, I want to thank my daughter, Linda, who devoted her invaluable time and exercised great patience to type the manuscript. She spent extensive hours on the layout of this book. Likewise, I would like to thank my son-in-law, Kevin, for designing the cover. It was a painstaking but marvelous job. In addition, I would like to thank Pastor Paul and Usha Watson who assisted in editing and writing a review. It was priceless. Also, I would like to thank Pastors Joe Persaud, Aubrey Greenidge and Dexter Burke who wrote reviews. Last but not least, the entire team at Parchment Global Publishing, for the final layout and publication of this book.

PREFACE

How this book came into fruition? For a very long time, my desire to write focused on two broad areas of interest. Yet I know that God would one day direct my thoughts of knowing what I should focus on. I have always been a strong advocate on great relationships, relationships that are founded on divine principles and godly living. My desire is to see that marriages are successful under God's direction; to see that families live together in harmony with each other: This can then be transferred to the church family as well as the community in which we live. The other area that was on my heart when it comes to writing was to see the need for believers to act responsibly in respect of their finances by fulfilling God's divine mandate in handling their finances with respect to their obligation to God, the local church, and the needs of people in their environment.

So now, let us get back to the question that I asked at the beginning of this book. How or why did this book come into fruition? As you read through the following pages, you will see that they hardly have anything to do with finances, but you will find somewhat a little on relationships. The idea for this book came while I was studying and meditating to see where the Lord was leading me to take the church in the last quarter of the year. Suddenly, the book of Ruth came to my mind.

As I was reading Chapter 1 of the Book of Ruth, I came to verses 16 and 17 which say, "*But Ruth replied, 'Don't urge me to leave you or to turn back from following you. Where you go I will go and where you stay I will stay. Your people will be my people and your God will be my God. Where you die I will die, and there I will be buried. May the Lord deal with me, be it ever so severely, if anything but death separates you and me.'* " I thought for a moment about what a remarkable statement that was made by this young lady. I prayed a little, and then as I continued in prayer, I heard

Dr Lawrence Chester

a voice saying to me, "This is your opportunity to write." So I asked, "Lord, what do you want me to write about? What is the topic?" The reply came, "Marvelous Hand." So this is the reason why the book is entitled, "The Marvelous Hand of God." Then the Lord went on to say that He wants the readers to understand that as He (The Lord) works through their lives, they will experience His Hand, and they will marvel and be in awe. So that is how this book came into existence.

DEDICATION

This book is dedicated to several people who have had an impact on my life. I dedicate this book to my beautiful and committed wife, Leila, of 40 years, to our three wonderful children Lisa, Linda, and Leary, my sons-in-law Alex and Kevin, and my four adorable grand-children Joshua, Jonathan, Aryana and Ava. Also to my brother, Dr. Victor Chester, who has had an early impact of Christianity on my life, Pastor Paul R. Watson and his wife, Usha, who are great advisors to me in my ministry, to Pastor Michael Persaud, who is my spiritual father and mentor, to my local church, Dayspring Bible Fellowship Church where I am proudly serving as Senior Pastor for the last seven years. Last but not least, this book is also dedicated to some of my very closest pastoral colleagues and friends in Christ; Joseph Persaud, Aubrey Greenidge, Stephen Gittens, Winfield Forde, Mahase Singh and Goucarran Singh.

INTRODUCTION

What you are about to glean over the next several pages of this book will be awesome and unforgettable. You will understand and find out that your present situation or circumstance should not determine your future success! Many times, our decisions are based upon our present circumstances. If they are favorable, then we are inclined to say the future is going to be bright. But, if circumstances are unfavorable, then we tend to go in reverse mode and ultimately push ourselves into depression. However, I want to encourage you to keep your eyes on the Lord and focus on Him because He will turn things around for you. After all, He is the miracle-working God! So, however disappointing and daunting the situation may seem, do not let it deter you from realizing your dreams, because whatever God has in store for you He will accomplish it.

I want to admonish you as you read these pages, be open to the Spirit of God because I know that the Lord will do marvelous things in your life. You will see how God took a little unknown Moabite girl and her situation (which at first seemed to be full of disappointments and failures), and He miraculously turned it around. <u>There is absolutely nothing too hard for God to do</u>! Remember what Isaiah said, *"To whom will you compare me? Or who is My equal? says the Holy One. Lift your eyes and look to the heavens: Who created all these? He who brings out the starry host one by one, and calls them each by name. Because of His great power and mighty strength not one of them is missing."* Isaiah 40: 25-26. *"Do you not know? Have you not heard? The Lord is the Everlasting God, the Creator of the ends of the earth. He will not grow tired or weary, and His understanding no one can fathom. He gave strength to the weary and increases the power of the weak."* Isaiah 40: 28-29. I am saying that there is no situation that you are facing today or will ever face in the future

Dr Lawrence Chester

that your God cannot handle! If God can name all the trillions of stars in the universe, He surely can handle your minute problem.

One of the main purposes of this book is to help those who are feeling discouraged, depleted or even depressed. The Lord will lift you out of your depression and take you to another level in you spiritual walk with Him. When you look back from where you came, you will see how marvelous the experience was. So, it is time to unlock the treasure house of God's amazing love and experience His providential Hand as you read through the pages of this book.

PART I
NAOMI'S DISAPPOINTMENT WAS RUTH'S DEVELOPMENT: RUTH 1:1-18.

When we focus on our disappointment, we eventually find ourselves in a state of depression. We are actually setting up ourselves for failure and defeat. Many people do not move forward in their endeavor to become successful because of the vision of looming failures that keep coming up before them. What many people do not recognize is that if there is no disappointment or failure, then there will be no area for God to work through. So when we face situations and difficulties beyond our control, we need to make contact with Jesus Christ, "The Master of Disaster." Naomi's disappointments became the platform for Ruth's development.

CHAPTER ONE
DECISION TIME

> *Our plan can change in a moment's time, especially when God is working. The best part is, God does it for His honor but He also does it for our benefit.*

Elimelech's decision to take his family to Moab was solely an economic decision. And, just to point out, nothing was wrong with that because we all need to provide for our families economically. Sometimes, decisions are made out of alignment with the will of God and also to satisfy our own selfish desires. I am originally from Guyana, South America, a small country being bordered by Brazil on the South, Venezuela on the West and Suriname on the East. I migrated with my family to the United States in 1992. However, our stay was a short one because we felt that the Lord wanted us to return to Guyana to help train the young pastors. Around that time, many of the more experienced pastors had already migrated to the United States. My point is that many people make different decisions based on varying circumstances.

Elimelech's decision was based solely on the fact that there was a famine in Bethlehem. He made a choice to go to Moab, even though it was a temporary one. *"In the days when the Judges ruled, there was a famine in the land, and a man from Bethlehem Judah, together with his wife and two sons, went to live for a while in the country of Moab. The man's name was Elimelech, his wife's name Naomi, and the names of his two sons were Mahlon and Kilion. They were Ephrathites from Bethlehem, Judah. And they went to Moab and lived there."* Ruth 1: 1-2. Now some explanation is needed to clarify the origin of the Moabites.

In the book of Genesis, chapter 19 and verse 37, we learned that Lot ended up sleeping with his two daughters. He committed incest and so the older daughter became the ancestress of Moab. Ever since that time, there have been intermittent peace and conflict between the Israelites and the Moabites. The connection is clear that Ruth was a descendant of Moab. It was during one of the peaceful interchanges between Israel and Moab that Elimelech decided to go down to Moab because of the famine in Bethlehem. The meaning of Elimelech's name is, "My God is King" and Naomi's name means, "Pleasant." So, "My God is King" was married to "Miss Pleasant." This seemed to be a beautiful romantic and spiritual correlation of unity. Nothing could have been going better for the couple. They were enjoying life together, or so it seemed.

What Elimelech did not realize was the fact that God was about to break in on the scene. He did not realize that his decision to go to Moab was actually directed by God. He went for economic reasons but God was about to turn it around for His honor and glory. As a matter of fact, Naomi ended up staying much longer in Moab than she anticipated. No one knows for sure how long the famine lasted in Bethlehem. I am pretty sure that Elimelech's idea was to make a quick turnaround in Moab and then head back to Bethlehem. Our plan can change in a moment's time, especially when God is working. The best part is, <u>God does it for His honor but He also does it for our benefit</u>. Elimelech made a selfish decision to go, but God broke in on the scene and started a phenomenal experience and journey for a young lady who would become the focal point and heroine of this amazing story. So when God has a plan, it does not matter how He gets it done, but He will get it done by all means, whether He has to take us through the fire, earthquakes or windy storms. Just remember, He is God. <u>He does the possible through the impossible</u>! He makes impossible looks so possible you would look back and never thought it was possible. Now, the events will unfold as we delve and dig deeper into this powerful story of God's Amazing Grace!

CHAPTER TWO
THE DISAPPOINTMENT OF NAOMI

> *Many people get weak and welter under the storm, but we need to rise above the storm and be a victor instead of a victim!*

It does not matter if your name means, "Miss Pleasant" as in Naomi's case or "Miss Perfect." When troubles hit, they can come to anyone regardless whether we are rich or poor, talented or not talented. No race is exempted, no one is exempted! When hurricane Katrina made landfall in the United States on August 29th, 2005, the winds stretched some 400 miles across the Atlantic moving eastward. It brought sustained winds of 100 – 140 miles per hour. It was the third strongest and largest hurricane to make landfall in the history of the United States. In New Orleans, the levees were designed for a category three, but Katrina peaked at a category five with up to 175 miles per hour. The final death toll was one thousand eight hundred and thirty-six. Primarily, one thousand five hundred and seventy-seven for Louisiana and two hundred and thirty-eight for Mississippi. More than half of the victims were senior citizens. The storm's surge was 20 feet high. At one time, there were 705 people still missing. The hurricane affected more than fifteen million people in different ways. Some had to evacuate their homes, some were affected with higher gas prices and the economy was suffering. An estimated 80% of New Orleans was under water with up to 20 feet deep in certain places. Hurricane Katrina caused 81 billion dollars in damages to properties and a total of 150 billion dollars in damages in both Louisiana and Mississippi (Wikipedia 2005). Everyone suffered, no one in that region was exempted.

When hurricane Sandy hit in October 2012 in New York City, the President himself issued a state of emergency for New York. The New York Stock Exchange was shut down, New York tunnels, bridges, and subways were all closed. Mayor Bloomberg warned that Sandy was the storm of the century. Over eight million New Yorkers have different memories for that fateful night when Sandy's storm's surge slammed against the city's shore causing billions of dollars in damages, plunging the city into darkness and ultimately killing 43 people (Wikipedia 2012). The Battery Park on lower Manhattan remained under water for four days. My point is, when problems come, they can hit us all. Everyone in the path of the storm was hit and affected. As in the case of Naomi, she experienced a bad situation in her life. This was truly a terrible disappointment. Obviously, she did not handle it very well. Like so many people today, when trouble hits, they do not handle it or respond very well. Many people get weak and welter under the storm, but we need to rise above the storm and be a victor instead of a victim!

"Now Elimelech, Naomi's husband, died, and she was left alone with her two sons." Ruth 1:3. Loneliness can be a very troubling experience and can lead to despair. Eventually, after some time had elapsed, her two boys whose name means, "Sickly" and "Pining" respectively, both married two Moabite women. Killion, whose name means "Pining" was married to Orpah whose name means "Long-Neck" or "girl with a full mane or rain cloud." The reason I am mentioning names with their meanings is because, the meaning of a name can have negative or positive effect on our lives. You will see what effect their names had on their lives. It is recorded in the book of Ruth Chapter 1 and verses 4 and 5 that both boys died. Naomi not only lost her husband, but now she lost both of her sons. The fact of the matter is that Naomi's disappointment really took a toll on her. You will see how this bitter disappointment and loss caused her to make some poor decisions. If your life is not planted in God, when disappointments and sorrows come, they can drive you into a state of depression. Let me remind you that when disappointment, discouragement and despondency face us, we need to cast our cares upon Jesus because He cares for us! The Bible tells us in the book of Jeremiah that, "God's hand is not short that He

cannot save neither His ear heavy that He cannot hear." What I did not mention to you earlier is that Ruth's name means, "Friendship," and very soon she would become the true friend of Naomi in the time of her greatest trial.

We all need a friend in our lives especially when dark days are upon us or when we feel like those days are looming around. This friendship would soon become the turning point for Naomi. Ruth was a Moabite woman whom many would have passed over as insignificant and would not have recognized, especially those from Bethlehem. We find these kinds of scenarios today in our church world. We tend to look at the negative that come out of people and degrade them, rather than try to help them to improve their lives positively with the help of Jesus Christ. This young lady, Ruth saw an opportunity and ran after it. She did not hesitate to do so because she saw something special.

Naomi's heart and mind became blinded by the physical as is illustrated by the following passage. *"Then Naomi said to her two daughters-in-law, 'Go back each of you to your mother's home. May the Lord show kindness to you, as you have shown to your dead and to me. May the Lord grant that each of you will find rest in the home of another husband.' Then she kissed them and they wept aloud and said to her, 'We will go back with you to your people.' But Naomi said, 'Return home, my daughters. Why would you come with me? Am I going to have any more sons, who could become your husbands? Return home, my daughters; I am too old to have another husband. Even if I thought there was still hope for me - even if I had a husband tonight and then gave birth to sons - would you wait until they grew up? Would you remain unmarried for them? No, my daughters. It is more bitter for me than for you because the Lord's hand has gone out against me!'"* Ruth 1:8-13. Naomi was just looking more at the material side of things and what actually happened. She started accusing God of leaving and forsaking her. She was living in the past. If we dwell in the past like Naomi did, the past will hurt us especially if it is not good.

Naomi, like many people today, was living in the flesh which means she was trusting the physical rather than trusting in God. Her life was basically in the material. Her faith was weak even though she was supposed to be a pleasant person. Many people today are living disappointed lives because they focus on the physical, material and natural. God wants us to see beyond this material and physical world, beyond what our mind is comprehending right now. Everything Naomi said was true according to the natural way as she looked at her situation. But the Lord wants us to see life differently! The material man cannot comprehend the things of God because they are spiritually discerned. The Bible clearly tells us in Hebrews Chapter 11 and verse 6, *"And without faith it is impossible to please God..."* It takes more than seeing in the natural or depending on the things of this world. As a matter of fact, we have to put on spiritual eyes to see God and spiritual ears to hear from God. Sadly, Naomi allowed the death of her husband and the death of her two sons to devour her faith.

CHAPTER THREE
THE DIVERSION OF ORPAH

> *Do not ever allow another person's disappointment to deter, distract or dampen your goals and aspirations, and especially your faith in our Lord and Savior, Jesus Christ!*

The verse that really struck me that shows Orpah's reluctance in moving forward with her life and with confidence in God's will is verse 14 of Chapter 1. *"At this they wept again. Then Orpah kissed her mother-in-law goodbye, but Ruth clung to her."* Let me elaborate here a little on Orpah's diversion. You see, Orpah was distracted by Naomi's disappointment. The long talk that Naomi had with Orpah sent her faith and confidence spiraling downwards. We have to be very careful in our Christian walk because if we are not, it becomes very easy for us to be distracted and discouraged by others. When you listen to the wrong people and associate with the wrong crowd, you would soon find yourself heading in the wrong direction and your walk with Christ will be regressive and your faith dampened. Just a couple of hours or days earlier, Orpah was ready to move forward, but the words which were sown into her caused her to change her mind and she became distracted and went backwards. Do not ever allow another person's disappointment to deter, distract or dampen your goals and aspirations, and especially your faith in our Lord and Savior, Jesus Christ! Always remember, Philippians Chapter 1 and verse 6 says, *"Being confident of this, that He Who began a good work in you will carry it on to completion."*

It is one thing to set out on a course, but yet another thing to maintain that course. Think about a ship setting sail, even though turbulent waves may hit, it has to stay on its course until it reaches its destination! We always have to be on the guard with our lives when the enemy of our souls tries to catch us off guard to divert us off course. Satan's plan and purpose is to, "steal, kill and destroy" our dreams and hinder us from reaching our goals and destinations. God does not give everything to us with a gold spoon because <u>HE WANTS US TO TRUST HIM</u> even in the difficult times. As we move on to the next chapter, you will see the difference between the two young ladies, Orpah and Ruth. While one was distracted by the words of discouragement, the other was determined to move on with the wisdom of development.

Demas was not only a co-worker with the Apostle Paul but he was also a very close friend. But Demas allowed the world with its allurements and attractions to devour him. He is described in 2 Timothy Chapter 4, verse 10 as one who loves this world, *"For Demas, because he loved this world, has deserted me and has gone to Thessalonica."* Obviously, Paul was not pleased with Demas's decision. Because, instead of staying on course with Paul, he diverted and went into the wrong direction. Does it sound strange to us when people divert out of the way? I remember as a young Christian growing up, a few of my close friends diverted out of the way of following Christ. They took the path of least resistance and failed to continue to walk in the ways to which God had called them. You see, Orpah could have had a great future, but she diverted, went back and nothing was heard of her again. So, I want to encourage you not to be discouraged by the negative things you hear, you should only be inclined to obey the Holy Spirit by listening to Him and the people He brings along your pathway. Eventually, as you continue to be obedient and continue to walk in the light that God shines on the way, you will experience victory! The sad truth is that many people who are doing exactly what Orpah did, will find themselves going backward. In other words, they will not accomplish what the Lord intends for them to accomplish because their eyes are not fixed on Jesus. The cares of this life come in and choke the good word out of their hearts. Ultimately, their minds become filled with fear, doubt, defeat and discouragement. My exhortation to you would be to get back into focus, just in case you have drifted. <u>Always keep your eyes on Jesus</u>! Hebrews Chapter 12, verse 2, *"Let us fix our eyes on Jesus, the Author and Perfector of our faith..."*

CHAPTER FOUR
THE DETERMINATION OF RUTH

> *If you allow your problems and petty situations to govern you, it will become difficult for you to see your real potential.*

Naomi is supposedly one of those, "experienced Christians" who knows the word of God, who has been in Church all of his or her life, maybe singing in the choir, teaching a Sunday School class and possibly a Senior Advisor to the Pastor. But suddenly, all that Naomi had learned and been taught in all the previous years leading up to this awful time in her life was lost. She lost her husband and her two sons and could not face the reality of loneliness. As a result, this plunged her into deep despondency. However, that which seemed to be the dark and disappointing reality for Naomi became the dawn of Ruth's incredible destiny. Naomi sees disappointment, Ruth sees her destiny.

Like so many people today, faced with disappointment that they had never seen before, and as the saying goes, "when it rains, it pours," Naomi experienced the bitterest time of her life. If you are faced today with bitterness and sorrow, or if your life is in turmoil and the only thing you are seeing is darkness and disappointment, I have good news for you. Try to adopt the attitude of Ruth and begin to see your destiny as a bright one; a future ahead of you that God has designed and no one can hinder you from experiencing the Marvelous Hand of God. Jerimiah 29:11 states, *"For I know the plans I have for you declares the Lord, plans to prosper you and not to harm you, plans to give you Hope and a future."*

Ruth 1:14 says, *"Ruth clung to her."* Another translation says, *"she cleave unto Naomi."* Ruth glued herself to Naomi. What Naomi could not see in herself, Ruth saw. Naomi was clouded by her problems and she lost focus of whom she really was. If you allow your problems and petty situations to govern you, it will become difficult for you to see your real potential. Let me remind you that both Orpah and Ruth made sincere pledges to follow Naomi, to build a life that would last for a lifetime, but only Ruth kept her promise. If you are in a relationship with Christ, or as a matter of fact, a relationship with anyone, or even your church, and you are faced with problems beyond your control, I have one simple advice for you; adopt the Ruth Principle. Glue yourself to your partner if it is marriage, glue yourself to your church if it is a church organization, or if it is friendship, glue yourself to your friend. Do not leave, just cleave.

Naomi had lost hope. All she was thinking about was earthly because she tried once more to persuade Ruth to go back. Ruth 1:15 says, *"'Look,' said Naomi, 'your sister-in-law is going back to her people and her gods. Go back with her.'"* Is this not exactly what so many Christians do? They imitate the crowd that is taking the path of least resistance. It is so easy to return to the "attractions" that you were once engaged in. It is really not that difficult to detour into a detrimental state. Naomi, who really should have known better, was really not showing a good example to Ruth. But this young lady saw tremendous potential in Naomi and her God. You see, Ruth must have done some homework by reading about her great uncle Abraham's faith. She must have read about Abraham, being a friend of God. Something extraordinary was beginning to stir up inside of her. Her faith was expanding day by day. So even though she was persuaded to leave and go back into idolatry, her commitment to stay with Naomi was permanent. But Ruth replied, *"Don't urge me to leave you or turn back from you. Where you go I will go, where you stay I will stay. Your people will be my people and your God my God. Where you die I will die, and there I will be buried. May the Lord deal with me, be it ever, so severely, if anything but death separates you and me."* Ruth 1:16-17. This was a genuine determination of a young lady who saw immense potential in Naomi, even though Naomi could not see it herself.

Ruth came to the point in her life that only death could separate or sever her from her destiny. May I take the liberty to ask you these two questions? What is keeping you back from your destiny? Do you have any obstacles that are hindering you? The Apostle Paul wrote convincingly when he said, *"Who shall separate us from the love of Christ? Shall trouble, or hardship or persecution or famine or nakedness or danger or sword? No, in all these things we are more than conquerors through Him who loved us. For I am convinced that neither death nor life, neither angels nor demons, neither the present nor the future, nor any powers, neither height nor depth, nor anything else in all creation, will be able to separate us from the love of God that is in Christ Jesus our Lord."* Romans 8:35-39. I do not know about you, but I think that the Apostle Paul must have learned something from this young girl, Ruth. Ruth lived and experienced exactly what Paul was talking about. She did not allow the death of her husband to separate her from the love of God. Also, Ruth did not allow the diversion of her sister-in-law, Orpah to set her back in the wrong direction. She did not allow the constant discouragement of Naomi to deter or dampen her desires. She moved forward with God! When our focus is on the Lord, we will conquer our enemies. When we are determined like Ruth was, nothing can stop us! As a matter of fact, even if you are distracted or you are faced with a detour, you can be victorious as long as your eyes are fixed on the goal and you, "set your face like a flint" as is expressed in the book of Isaiah. Junior Tucker expressed it beautifully in his song, "I'm determined to fulfil my destiny, I'm determined to defeat my enemy, I am determined to walk in victory..."

PART II
RUTH ENGAGED IN HER DESTINY: RUTH 1:19 - 2:1-22.

Naomi's bitterness and frustration never impacted Ruth's life negatively. When Naomi left Bethlehem to go to Moab, evidently she was in better spirits. She seemed to have had everything under control. It may have appeared that way because of the exclamation made by the women of the town. They exclaimed in Ruth 1:19c, *"Can this be Naomi?"* Could this be the same wonderful worshipper and committed Christian we all know? People do change when they are faced with unfavorable circumstances. People react differently under pressure; Naomi evidently was no exception. She called herself "bitter" and became very angry. Naomi's demeanor was clearly evident. Naomi's burden was so heavy to carry at this moment, but that never distracted Ruth from realizing God's appointment. Ruth's faith saw what Naomi's faith could not have seen. Ruth saw a harvest coming her way. In this section of the book we will explore what Ruth did to realize her destiny. We all need to focus on engaging and achieving our destiny.

CHAPTER FIVE
RUTH PURSUED HER DESTINY

> *Our minds are fogged up with the disappointment. We need to look beyond the dark clouds and start looking for the rainbow and enjoy the sunshine and beautiful sky.*

The Scripture records the following account. "*So the two women went on until they came to Bethlehem. When they arrived in Bethlehem, the whole town was stirred because of them, and the women exclaimed, 'Can this be Naomi?' 'Don't call me Naomi,' she told them. 'Call me Mara, because the Almighty has made my life very bitter. I went away full but the Lord has brought me back empty. Why call me Naomi? The Lord has afflicted me; the Almighty has brought misfortune upon me.' So Naomi returned from Moab accompanied by Ruth, the Moabitess, her daughter in law, arriving in Bethlehem as the barley harvest was beginning.*" Ruth 1: 19-22. Naomi was so bitter and angry with God that she became very frustrated over her disappointment. Sadly, she even accused God of afflicting her.

Many people in the world today are guilty of doing exactly what Naomi did. When things do not go the way they expect it to go, or when their plans are interrupted suddenly and life starts hitting them with negative events that seem out of control, they throw their hands up in disgust and despair and accuse God of not being there for them. Many people want God's leadership but they only want Him to lead them on their terms and conditions. My question to you would be, "If your desire is to lead your own life and make your own decisions, then why ask God for

His leadership?" You have to realize, it does not matter how God leads, what matters most is that you will eventually reach your destination the way God designed it for you!

None of us is in any place to make accusations against God. After all, most of the time, if not all the time, we set out to make our own decisions in our lives. The problem with that is, when they do not turn out well for us, we tend to blame it on someone else and even God gets the blame. Several years earlier, Elimelech made a decision to go to Moab because of the economic conditions that were not favorable in Bethlehem and that decision did not turn out well for him and his family. He died along with his two sons, hence leaving his wife a widow. Many times, when we suffer loss, we do not see beyond the loss. Our minds are fogged up with the disappointment. We need to look beyond the dark clouds and start looking for the rainbow and enjoy the sunshine and beautiful sky. Just remember that your God has everything under His control and in His Marvelous Hand.

Naomi called herself "bitter" and went into a complaining mode. Does that sound familiar to any of us? We may choose to become bitter, resentful and negative and the list can go on and on. Never allow yourself to become so bitter and resentful because you can miss the glory and warmth of the sunshine of God's plan for your life. The dark clouds of sorrow and sickness can quickly overwhelm us, and when it does, the cry of sadness and the mourning of losses can overtake us. So let us remain positive and up-beat and you will know, without a doubt, that God has a plan working out for you. <u>His plan for you is bright, bold and beautiful</u>, but in order for you to see and experience it, you have to look at life from a different perspective. You need new "spiritual" eyes. Your old vision is clouded with fear and doubt and it is blocking and hindering you from accessing God's beauty. So let us all remain focused and keep pursuing our destiny because our dreams can become a reality like it did for Ruth. All we need is to put our faith into action and our God will do the rest.

Ruth not only fixed her eyes on the prize, but she exercised her faith in the person. *"And Ruth, the Moabitess said to Naomi, 'Let me go to the fields and pick up the left over grain behind anyone in whose eyes I find favor."* Ruth 2:2. Many people would like their dreams to be realized and they want God to lead them to their destiny, but their eyes are way off of Him and their faith is distracted by worldly attractions. Ruth was not sitting around idly and complaining about little problems like what so many of us do. If anyone has a reason to complain and grumble, it was Ruth. After all, her mentor, Naomi, was weak and weary. But Ruth's faith became so strong and steadfast that she exclaimed in verse 2 of Ruth Chapter 2, "*I am going to the fields.*" Her faith was put into action and you will learn very soon it paid off great dividends for her. Many people sit around and expect a "pie from the sky." They have what I call lazy faith instead of launching faith. But this young lady, Ruth, was so different from a lot of Christians who "grow up in church," but do not know how to tap into heaven's treasure house of faith. Ruth followed in the footsteps of Abraham, a man who believed God in his old age and became a great patriarch. So obviously, she was not going to allow this promise to slip by easily. You too can position yourself and pursue your destiny despite all difficulties and dangers you may face. It may look very dark and gloomy, but have patience because your God has promises that are not yet unfolded for you to access. Just remember you can be your own hindrance. Do not divert like Orpah because she missed the opportunity for her blessings. Your God desires better things for you and will certainly take you to better places. Be determined like Ruth was because you will reap great dividends like Ruth reaped. As you continue to read this book and move forward towards the Ruth phenomenon, you will experience God's Marvelous Hand in your life like it was in Ruth's life.

That which Naomi was frustrated over became a harvest of opportunity for Ruth. Most people like to see things done the easy way. But you know the old saying, "no pain no gain." Not everyone can handle disappointment. Anger, bitterness and resentment will soon step in to crush your dreams as in the case of Naomi. I want you to notice that Naomi, whose name means "pleasant," was the most annoying person to be around at this juncture of her life. However, Ruth whose name means "friendship," became a real and meaningful friend to Naomi. When people are going through rough patches in their lives and they are not handling it very well, they can certainly do with some real friendship. As Naomi focused on her disappointment, Ruth saw a dream coming to pass. This young lady was not deterred by any of the negative things she heard. You will also hear negative things, but never allow them to distract you from moving forward. As a matter of fact, Ruth's faith became stronger and stronger day by day. The more Naomi uttered negative words, the more Ruth's faith grew and became stronger.

I live in the Poconos in Pennsylvania. The temperatures in these last two last winters were many times in the negative. Living in subzero temperatures is not a pleasant experience. Many homes and businesses were adversely affected because of frozen and broken pipes. This would lead to a very high cost of repair. Not only that, but others have to pay very high heating bills. My point is, negative temperatures are not enjoyable. They are very painful both to the body and the wallet. Let us look also at negative bank accounts. People are being charged with fees by the bank. Those fees can be very high as well. Once again, negative bank accounts are very painful and embarrassing. There is nothing nice to enjoy about subzero temperatures and negative bank accounts. In both scenarios, they cost a lot of money and discomfort. In the spiritual sense also, negative words are very painful and discomforting. We are never blessed with such words.

In pursuing her dreams, Ruth's secret was obvious. She fixed her eyes on the prize and her "Lord and King." Hebrews 12:2 says, *"Let us fix our eyes on Jesus, the Author and Perfecter of our faith,…"* Ruth did not let go of Naomi, as I previously mentioned. Whatever it was that Ruth saw in her mentor, Naomi, it was difficult for Naomi to see because of all the negative things that were going on in her life. I want to remind you that as you are reading this book, do not allow your dreams and aspirations to be drenched and drowned by your disappointments and failures. I want to exhort you to keep your eyes on the "Perfector of your faith," and He will make all your dreams come to fruition and bring you into your destiny.

CHAPTER SIX
RUTH PRESSED INTO THE PRESENCE OF HER REDEEMER

> *Nothing in this world comes to stop you permanently, they are only temporary hindrances. Get up and push forward. Be an overcomer!*

The Scripture declares, *"Naomi said to her, 'Go ahead, my daughter.' So she went out and began to glean in the fields behind the harvesters. As it turned out, she found herself working in a field belonging to Boaz, who was from the clan of Elimelech."* Ruth 2:2b-3. It must be noted that Ruth arrived in Bethlehem during the time of barley harvest. This was the spring time, possibly during the month of April. Barley was the first grain that ripened in the spring. It was during this time that the first fruits of the earth were brought forth upon which the scriptures placed such great significance. "The time of barley harvest was a time of great joy and a time of great spiritual significance because it anticipated the great Redemptive work of Christ, His resurrection glory and the believer's eternal life in Christ." (Don Fontner on Ruth Series, Aug. 17th, 1993).

Barley harvest came just after a long winter. Please note that this young lady, Ruth, had a strong spiritual insight and deep understanding that around that time of the year, even though she was a Moabitess, she could enjoy freedom immediately in Bethlehem. She found herself in Bethlehem, the "House of Bread," the "House of Safety," and the

"House of Freedom." I pray that all believers who read this book would press on or push through their problems to experience the wonderful promises that are wrapped up in the power of the Gospel and the Epistles. The reason I am making such references is because you will see very shortly the significance of what took place in Ruth's life. She actually enveloped herself in her future, not by becoming complacent or indifferent but by pushing her way beyond the obstacles and hindrances that presented themselves before her. She knew that she would have to get past the obstacles and hindrances and this could have only been possible by being obedient to her master.

The latter part of Ruth Chapter 2 and verse 3 says, *"As it turned out, she found herself working in a field belonging to Boaz, who was from the clan of Elimelech."* (As mentioned earlier, Elimelech's name means, "my God is King"). Ruth's journey may not have been perfect, and some parts of your journey may not be perfect as well. But this time her action was very rewarding! "Miss Pleasant" (Naomi) who was her mentor found her way back and began to gain renewed spiritual insights. Naomi was awakened to the fact that Ruth was seeing something that she should have seen a long time ago. Have you ever been in a situation and you say to yourself, "I should have seen that coming, I knew it, I knew it." As one person puts it, "as long as there is life, there is hope." Ruth pressed toward the "mark of the high calling." Ruth invested in her future by getting in on, "the early rain." What do I mean? The first rain or early rain represents the first sowing in order to have an early reaping. Ruth Chapter 2 and verse 7b says, *"…she went into the field and has worked steadily from morning till now."* Ruth was completely sold out to work for Boaz even though, at that point in time, she did not realize what the end results would be. We must become faithful workers for the Lord even though we may not see what the results or rewards are immediately. But, I want to assure you that your rewards are on the way. I pray that you will remain focused and totally dedicated as Ruth. In the Lord's work, we should not succumb to the devices of the enemy, but rather we can take a short rest under the shelter of God's wings.

It is always very important to pay keen attention to the one who is mentoring you. When you do, the Lord will reveal His will and unfold His divine plan through them to you. Ruth came to Bethlehem which represents the "House of God." Barley harvest, as mentioned earlier, represents the believers overcoming their fears, their doubts and all kinds of obstacles and hindrances to the flesh. In Ruth's case, she had just lost her husband. To some people, this would have been a very bleak and dark situation. Maybe for Ruth it was, but only for a short time, because she did not allow the ongoing situation to set her back. In fact, she became an overcomer and she was strengthened by the Lord. Remember, as Willie Jolley said, "A setback is a setup for a comeback." If it is looking dark and gloomy for you, I want to assure you that the Lord will dispel the darkness with the powerful light of His Word. Everyone who is ready to be engaged in their destiny should be prepared to propel themselves into the presence of their redeemer. If Ruth could have done it during her time of adversity and became successful, you can do it despite your adverse situation! Do not allow anyone or anything to hinder you from moving forward in God's purpose for your life! Your miracle is right on the horizon! Never stop at the point that prevents you from your goal, it is only there as a temporary obstacle. Nothing in this world comes to stop you permanently, they are only temporary hindrances. Get up and push forward. Be an overcomer, it is barley harvest. Get in on the sowing and very soon you will be reaping. Pushing forward is very important. When a pregnant woman is asked to push and push, very soon before her is a brand new baby. Her pain and perseverance brought her a delightful sight, her baby boy or girl. Ruth had no time for gossip, she was busy gardening. We should take special note of this. We should be busy working the fields for the Lord and never get involved in laziness and indifference. Ruth pushed forward and propelled her way to her delightful destiny. We too can do the same if we want to be successful in the kingdom.

CHAPTER SEVEN

RUTH WAS PROTECTED BY HER REDEEMER

> *We must listen attentively and never be carried away or get side-tracked with the noise that can hinder us from hearing the voice of the Holy Spirit.*

As Ruth pursued her destiny and pushed her way closer and closer to her destination, she realized that she would need protection. *"So Boaz said to Ruth, 'My daughter, listen to me. Do not go and glean in another field and don't go away from here. Stay here with my servant girls. Watch the field where the men are harvesting, and follow along after the girls. I have told the men not to touch you. And whenever you are thirsty, go and get a drink from the water jars the men have filled.'"* Ruth 2:8-9. Ruth's protection came as a result of her complete obedience because she did not fail to listen and she did exactly what was asked of her. Our protection comes to us in similar circumstances if we find the art of listening and fully obeying God's commands whenever He speaks to us. The problem that many of us face is simply the fact that we are talking at the same time that God is speaking to us. When God, the Holy Spirit, speaks to us, He speaks in a still, small voice. Therefore, we must pay keen and careful attention. We must listen attentively and never be carried away or get side-tracked with the noise that can hinder us from hearing the voice of the Holy Spirit. The main reason Ruth was being blessed and protected was the fact that she learned early the art of listening to her Redeemer. Obviously, she had great spiritual insight into the things of

God. I pray that everyone who is pushing forward toward the realization of their destiny will also develop great listening skills by developing a spirit of discernment.

I am convinced that Ruth spent much time in studying about Moses and how he was protected by the Marvelous Hand of God. Moses declared in the book of Psalms Chapter 91 and verses 1 and 2, *"He who dwells in the shelter of the Most High will rest in the shadow of the Almighty. I will say of the Lord, He is my refuge and my fortress, my God, in whom I trust."* Jesus made a very profound statement when He said the following, *"My Sheep listen to my voice; I know them, and they follow me. I give them eternal life, and they shall never perish; no one can snatch them out of my hand. My Father, who has given them to me, is greater than all; no one can snatch them out of my Father's hand."* John 10: 27-29. What compelling and powerful words from our Lord Himself! These are words of comfort and protection, without any reservation whatsoever. Jesus is declaring to the world that He and the Father are One as stated in John Chapter 10 and verse 30. If you only knew the eternal power and the eternal authority that your Lord has, then you will have no problem, no hesitation and no doubt to place yourself under His everlasting wings of protection. Ruth found out very quickly that she could place herself under the mighty hand of God. You must understand that Boaz is a type of Christ. So, when Ruth trusted Boaz for her protection, she was actually trusting Jesus! If we could only grasp in a small way what Ruth did and adopt this principle, we would be able to face life a lot easier. The problem with the majority of Christians today is that they are not releasing their problems into His Hands, instead they are walking around with sad faces as if they have the world of problems on their heads. As a result of this, the enemy of their souls quickly comes in with discouragement which ultimately brings failure to many of them. I want to exhort you to keep your eyes on "El Shaddai" because that is exactly what this young lady did, and she was totally protected.

As I close this chapter, I want to remind you of the authority of God's Holy Word. It will also take some faith on your part to stay protected and safe. In Daniel Chapter 3, we read about the account of the three Hebrew boys who were commanded to bow down to the golden image that King Nebuchadnezzar had made. The boys emphatically refused to bow down to the image but it took faith on their part to refuse. "*If we are thrown into the blazing furnace, the God we serve is able to save us from it, and He will rescue us from your hand, O King.*" Dan 3:17. In the end, they were all saved. It took faith in the Power of God and they were protected from the awful hand of the enemy by the Marvelous Hand of God. My point here is, when you seem to be facing fires from the hand of the enemy, do not panic, just trust your Lord by placing complete faith in Him. I believe it was Corrie Ten Boon who said, "There is no panic in heaven, only plans."

CHAPTER EIGHT
RUTH WAS PROVIDED FOR BY HER REDEEMER

> *People may always have doubts about you and may even avoid and scorn you, but your God will turn your sorrowful situation into a sweet sentiment!*

Let us look back at Ruth Chapter 2 and verse 9. *"Watch the field where the men are harvesting, and follow along after the girls. I have told the men not to touch you. And whenever you are thirsty, go and get a drink from the water jars the men have filled."* As Ruth pursued and pushed towards her destiny, she was not only protected from the evils of the surrounding environment but she was totally provided for by her imminent redeemer. This is a picture of the utter amazement of God's grace upon her life! She was despised because of her background. Remember she is a descendant of Lot who committed incest with his older daughter who became the ancestress of Moab. So Ruth had a questionable past, just like many today who have a shameful and shackled past. But you do not have to be moved or disillusioned by your past. The Blood of Jesus Christ, God's Son, cleanses from all sin! Be reminded that Jesus died for all of our sins and that is what makes the Grace of God so amazing! People may always have doubts about you and may even avoid and scorn you, but your God will turn your sorrowful situation into a sweet sentiment! When you totally surrender everything to Him, He will certainly make a positive change within your life and turn your hurtful condition into hallelujah praise. The latter part of verse 9 says, *"Whenever you are thirsty, go get a drink from the water jars, the men have filled."* Ruth did not even have to fill her water pot; everything was done for her by someone else. You and I who are children of the King of kings and Lord of lords, will have all of our needs supplied. Even if He have to use others to do it, He will use them because everything belongs to God anyway.

Ruth was not only under "El Shaddai's" protection but now she was experiencing what I call "Jehovah Jireh." Ruth's secret to being provided for was simply the fact that <u>she was not a worrier but a worshipper</u>! Too many of us worry over everything, we even worry over the things we cannot change. We need to be reminded and pray the "Serenity Prayer," which states, "God, grant me the serenity to accept the things I cannot change, courage to change the things I can and wisdom to know the difference." We need to worship more and evidently, our needs will be met. I really do not know how God will do it, but one thing I do know, it will be done. *"At this, she bowed down with her face to the ground. She exclaimed, 'Why have I found such favor in your eyes that you notice me a foreigner?'"* Ruth 2:10. As you will see, when you truly worship God (worship God in Spirit and in Truth) and acknowledge Him as the Creator of the universe and the originator and executioner of salvation, it does not matter what nationality you are or from what background, <u>our Lord and Savior loves all and wants to redeem all</u>. When you are saved and transformed by His Holy power, through the blood of Jesus Christ, you now have a new name, a new identity, a new image and a new purpose! Ruth, being a Moabitess, did not change the fact that God would love her and that He would accept adoration from her. Similarly, whoever you are and whatever you have done in your past will not change the fact that your God loves you and will save you.

Let us dig a little deeper into Ruth's provision. In Ruth Chapter 2 and verse 12, it says, *"May the Lord repay you for what you have done. May you be richly rewarded by the Lord, the God of Israel, under whose wings you have come to take refuge."* Ruth did not say good bye to her mother-in-law, as Orpah did, instead, in the most difficult times, when it seemed like all hell would break loose for Naomi, Ruth stood by Naomi's side! After all, Ruth's name which means "friendship," really showed what a true and genuine friend would do during such times of darkness. Many times, the person you least expect to show kindness is the one who shows up the best. So, never count anyone out because God can use anyone to accomplish His purpose and will in your life.

We have seen it over and over again throughout Bible times. Let me give you a few examples of my own experience when God used people to provide for me when I least expected it. I remember in 1992 when I was venturing out to start a new business; I was still living in Guyana, South America, where I am from originally and I needed some funds to do some purchasing for the business. So, one of my neighbors who had recently moved into the neighborhood came over to see me. During the discussion our jobs came up, and so money came into the discussion. My neighbor looked at me and said, "I will loan you 25,000.00(USD)." Yes, it was $25,000.00! Even though he hardly knew me, he made that offer. All that I could have said in great astonishment was, "thank you!" From that day forward, he granted me soft loans on various occasions. It was not only him but his father also funded my business. It got even better when one of his brothers rented me one of his properties to do my business at a very large discounted rate. This is what I call the "Marvelous Hand of God!" More recently, since living in North East Pennsylvania, USA, I faced a financial crisis in my life and three of my friends came to my assistance. All I knew then, was the fact that my God says that He will take care of all my needs according to His riches in glory.

Now let us take a closer look to further understand how this provision was made for Ruth. The main reason why Naomi and her family had moved to Moab was because of a famine in Bethlehem. But what they (Naomi and her family) did not realize was the setting up of what I call the "Ruth's phenomenon." The underlying purpose was for Naomi to meet Ruth. God used a famine in Bethlehem to bring about His purpose and His will. So eventually, God's Marvelous Hand was at work when He provided for Ruth, meeting all her needs through the man called Boaz who became her redeemer. So, Ruth not only found favor with Boaz, but she also flourished under him. Your life can flourish with God's favor and love if you are under His care. One thing Ruth learned was to trust the Lord. She was never frustrated even when things appeared to be looking desperate. She understood fully that she did not need to worry about the cares of this life and the various demands that came along.

I want to exhort you to have a similar approach when it comes to trusting your Lord to meet your needs. Matthew Chapter 6 and verses 25 through 34 give us the classic example of what it means to put your trust in the Lord. None of us who are born-again of the Spirit of God need to display any attitude of worry. As a matter of fact, when you worry, it does you no good and it also hurts your heavenly Father who cares for you, as is described in Matthew. When we worry, we are telling God, "Lord, here is a situation, (whether physical, financial or spiritual) which You cannot handle!" We reach a place where we put God in a box and we try to limit Him. Your God and my God is greater than any situation or circumstance. Proverbs Chapter 3 and verses 5 and 6 say, *"Trust in the Lord with all your heart and do not lean on your own understanding. In all your ways acknowledge Him and He will direct your path."*

PART III
RUTH ENTRUSTED HERSELF FULLY UNDER BOAZ: RUTH 2:13-23.

The story of Ruth is now beginning to build great momentum. When Ruth focused her eyes on the goal which was intended for her from day one of this incredible journey, there was absolutely no turning back. No one even dared to prevent her or stand in the way. Her determination was so intense, and her commitment level was set at such a high bar, that everyone who came into contact with her was amazed at her discipline. It was no coincidence that she fixed her eyes on her destiny as it was done with all her might and will; Ruth fell into the hands of her Redeemer. Notice that her redeemer had no hesitation in performing the task of full protection and provision for her.

Our Lord does the same for those of us who are His children; those of us who are dedicated in reaching our goals and dreams that are in alignment with His will and purpose. Clearly, when our thoughts are pure and holy, our Lord's Marvelous Hands will be upon us all the way through our journey. Ruth was fully blessed and was granted many favors, and obviously she had no reservation on her part to fully commit and entrust herself under Boaz's direction. What a beautiful statement that was made by Ruth. " *'May I continue to find favor in your eyes, my Lord,' she said, 'You have given me comfort and have spoken kindly to your servant. Though I do not have the standing as one of your servant girls.'* " Ruth 2:13. <u>We need to come to Christ just as we are (in our filthiness), and the Blood of Jesus will do the rest</u>! Finding God's favor to rest upon us should not be our problem. We need to submit ourselves to Him and God will grant us standing and favor!

Let me remind you of this incident in the book of Genesis Chapter 18 where the Angel of the Lord visited Abraham and told him that his wife Sarah would have a son at a specific time. Sarah laughed because her mind was in the flesh rather than in the spirit. She was limiting God's power to perform. In the same way, we find ourselves in similar situations doubting and limiting the miraculous power of God to operate in our dead circumstances! We are in no place to help ourselves, and rather than trusting the One who can, we find ourselves doubting and evidently we go with nothing. However, Ruth was definitely on a different level spiritually. She had no problem entrusting herself to Boaz. *"Trust in the Lord with all your heart and lean not on your own understanding, in all your ways acknowledge Him, and that He will make your paths straight."* Proverbs 3:5-6. Another translation says the Lord "directs your paths." This is what He did for Ruth and He will do the same for you if you allow Him to do it.

CHAPTER NINE
RUTH ENCOUNTERED PEACE

> *The secret to have peace in this turbulent world, which is always in conflict and confusion, is to rest completely in the Presence of our Lord and Savior, Jesus Christ!*

"At meal time Boaz said to her, " 'Come over here' " Ruth 2:14a. This was an assurance of peace. In other words, do not worry yourself over anything. Do not get yourself clogged up with the burdens of the day. Do not get entangled with the affairs of this life. After all, <u>Jesus is the Author of life. He would like for you to spend time with Him, which can become invaluable and priceless.</u> The Bible tells us in Isaiah Chapter 55 and verse 1, *"Come all you who are thirsty, come to the waters; and you who have no money, come and eat! Come, buy wine and milk, without money and without cost."* Four times in this verse God is beckoning to us, "Come." It is a free invitation to come to Him. May I remind you that Boaz is an Old Testament figure of Christ. So the invitation by Boaz to Ruth to "come over here" is similar to what Christ is saying to us. This is an assurance of peace. Jesus said, *"... In this world you will have trouble. But take heart! I have overcome the world."* John 16:33b. Jesus also said, *"Come to me, all you who are weary and burdened, and I will give you rest. Take My yoke upon you and learn from Me, for I am gentle and humble in heart, and you will find rest for your souls."* Matthew 11:28-29. This is exactly the kind of peace that Ruth received and experienced. Imagine her entire demeanor was relaxed and serene. The secret to have peace in this turbulent world which is always in conflict and confusion is to <u>rest</u>

completely in the Presence of our Lord and Savior, Jesus Christ! Another great quotation from Jesus is taken from the book of John's Gospel. *"Peace I leave with you; My peace I give to you. I do not give to you as the world gives. Do not let your hearts be troubled and do not be afraid."* John 14:27. What a scene it was for Ruth! What an experience of stability and comfort, knowing she possessed the kind of peace that calmed her mind and body! This can be an awesome experience for all who have been troubled with discomfort and pain, knowing that the Prince of Peace lives in us. When Jesus lives in our hearts, then we know, without a shadow of a doubt, that fear is gone, unbelief is eradicated, and God's beautiful peace has taken complete control of our lives. A life that was once shaky and turbulent is now travelling on serene waters.

CHAPTER TEN
RUTH WAS ENRICHED WITH COMPANIONSHIP

> *There are several chapters of our lives that God leads us into. But there is one final chapter where He will catapult us into that which will be very remarkable, refreshing and unforgettable!*

"… 'Have some bread and dip it in the wine vinegar.' When she sat down with the harvesters, he offered her some roasted grain. She ate all she wanted and had some left over." Ruth 2:14. Ruth is not only encountering peace, but is now having an enriched companionship! <u>Jesus is our dependable and durable companion.</u>

Many people are easily deceived with the flattery of others. Hence, they fall to the wild schemes and cunning plans of the enemy of their souls. Ruth was offered bread which is symbolic of the body of our Lord Jesus Christ. In John Chapter 6 and verses 48 through 51, Jesus said "*I am the Bread of Life. Your forefathers ate the manna in the desert, yet they died. But here is the bread that comes down from heaven, which a man may eat and not die. I am the living Bread that came down from heaven. If anyone eats of this bread, he will live forever…*" Now, I do hope your understanding is opening to the fact that this was no ordinary companionship that Ruth entered in because she was having real fellowship and companionship with the "Bread from heaven," who is the Son of God. If you would desire to have such a great companionship in your life right now, just invite the "Bread of life," Jesus Christ, into your heart. He is anxiously waiting to be invited in, and when you do so, you will see what an amazing and marvelous companionship this will be! This companionship is not only real, but it is also royal because you are coming to the King of all kings and Lord of all lords (who is in charge of this entire universe).

"But you are a chosen people, a royal priesthood, a holy nation, a people belonging to God, that you may declare the praises of Him who called you out of darkness into his wonderful light." I Peter 2:9. Hopefully, the light is getting brighter and it is becoming clearer for you to comprehend the kind of enrichment that Ruth was given. She was now royal and she was delivered from darkness! She moved forward from the land of Moab to the land of Bethlehem, the "House of Bread." Everyone can experience this royalty when they are converted to the Lord Jesus Christ. At first, we live <u>at the mercy of others</u>, but now we live <u>under the mercy of God</u>. The "House of Bread" is Bethlehem which also means "House of Mercy." The "Bread," represents Jesus, our companion, and the "Wine" represents the Holy Spirit who is our Comforter. This means the Holy Spirit comes forth with strength. So, when we are spiritually and emotionally depleted, the Holy Spirit who is our best friend comes to our aid and He strengthens and uplifts us! Ruth was experiencing strength through Boaz. Her life was now filled with true companionship when she was told by Boaz to "dip in the wine," which means you can totally depend on me (Boaz) to be your friend. If we all realize the kind of benefit that the Holy Spirit brings to our growth as a Christian, then we will not hesitate to make Him our best friend. The Holy Spirit brings complete care and satisfaction to every part of our beings. Jesus said, *"But I tell you the truth, it is for your good that I am going away. Unless I go away, the Counselor will not come to you; but if I go, I will send Him to you. When He comes, He will convict the world of guilt in regard to sin and righteousness and judgment."* John 16: 7-8. Then He went on further to say, *"I have much more to say to you more than you can now bear. But when He, the Spirit of Truth, comes, He will guide you into all truth. He will not speak on His own; He will speak only what He hears, and He will tell you what is yet to come."* John 16: 12-14.

This encounter that Ruth had with her redeemer was so remarkable and refreshing that it continued to catapult her closer and closer to her destiny. There are several chapters of our lives that God leads us into. But there is one final chapter where He will catapult us into that which will be very remarkable, refreshing and unforgettable! It is very important to be possessed by the Holy Spirit because "He is Truth," and when we possess Truth, we become contagious and our lives will affect others positively. I urge you right now to press on to be filled with the Holy Spirit in order for your "bread" to taste better. Bread of itself would not be complete, but bread with the compliment of wine is complete. Wine in the Old Testament is typically used with a meal, but in the New Testament it is used as a disinfectant and for medical purposes. Therefore my deduction is that the Holy Spirit when infilling us, disinfects our souls from all sins and heals our bodies of all diseases!

Jesus gave us a very fascinating, but compelling story of real compassion. *"In reply Jesus said, 'A man was going down from Jerusalem to Jericho, when he fell into the hands of robbers. They stripped him of his clothes, beat him and went away, leaving him half dead. A priest happened to be going down the same road, and when he saw the man, he passed by on the other side. So too, a Levite, when he came to the place and saw him, passed by on the other side. But a Samaritan, as he travelled came where the man was; and when he saw him, he took pity on him. He went to him and bandaged his wounds, pouring on oil and wine. Then he put the man on his own donkey, took him to an inn and took care of him The next day he took out two silver coins and gave them to the inn keeper.'Look after him,' he said, 'and when I return, I will reimburse you for any extra expense you may have'"* Luke 10:30-35. This story so strongly illustrates what takes place in many religious organizations in our world today. No doubt, there may be pastors and even worship leaders (Levites) who are not quite involved in the work of the Lord wholeheartedly. Instead, they may be in it for their own gain. But I strongly suggest, if you are not binding up the wounds of the hurting and those who are suffering in one way or another, seek the face of God and ask him to give you a compassionate heart. As illustrated in the Scriptures in Luke Chapter 10 and verse 34, wine and oil are mentioned. The wine and oil represent the Holy Spirit. I urge you to earnestly seek to be filled with the Holy Spirit because when He inhabits you, then the pressing needs around you will become easier to identify and difficult to ignore. In Philippians Chapter 1 verses 15 through 18, Paul the Apostle condemned some who were preaching for selfish reasons. But he also said that even if someone were doing it for selfish reasons, God will still honor His Word. Obviously, the priest and the Levite only looked good on the outside but had no inward experience. They were empty on the inside. The Samaritan, on the other hand, who was supposed to be an outcast, evidently had some sort of inward change in his life to perform such a good deed. My whole point on this matter is, when you have an enriching relationship with the Lord Jesus Christ, you will go to deeper depths and higher heights with Him. Ruth was the person who had such a great internal relationship with the Lord, even though she was from Moab. You can clearly see that, <u>God is no respecter of persons</u>. He will fill and use anyone who is responsive to His Truth.

CHAPTER ELEVEN
RUTH ENDEAVORED TO BE BLESSED AND STAYED BLESSED

> *Our Heavenly Father warns us not to worry about the cares of this life. When our God has a blessing for us, He will seek us out to the very end.*

The Bible tells us the following account. "*So Ruth gleaned in the field until evening. Then she threshed the barley she had gathered, and it amounted to about an ephah. She carried it back to town, and her mother-in-law saw how much she had gathered. Ruth also brought out and gave her what she had left over after she had eaten enough. Her mother-in-law asked her, 'Where did you glean today? Where did you work? Blessed be the man who took notice of you!' Then Ruth told her mother-in-law about the one at whose place she had been working. 'The name of the man I worked with today is Boaz,' she said, 'the Lord bless him!' Naomi said to her daughter-in-law. 'He has not stopped showing his kindness to the living and the dead.' She added, 'That man is our close relative; he is one of our kinsman-redeemers.' Then Ruth the Moabitess said, 'He even said to me,' 'stay with my workers until they finish harvesting all my grain.' Naomi said to Ruth her daughter-in-law, 'It will be good for you, my daughter, to go with his girls, because in someone else's field you might be harmed.' So Ruth stayed close to the servant girls of Boaz to glean until the barley and wheat harvests were finished. And she lived with her mother-in-law.*" Ruth 2:17-23.

To comprehend more fully why Ruth persisted to be blessed and continued to be blessed, you must have a clear understanding of the meaning of "Barley" and "Wheat" harvest. Remember, this was the time when Ruth came to Bethlehem, which represents the "House of Bread" or "House of God." The barley harvest comes first in the spring and Ruth came just in time to sow into the kingdom. This is what I call "spiritual insight," recognizing the appropriate time to plant her seed. The barley harvest represents the first part of God's harvest. This harvest is referred to in Scripture as "overcomers." This harvest gives the believer the opportunity to rule and reign with Christ on the earth during the millennium. Evidently, Ruth represents the church ruling and reigning with Christ. Even though at this time, Ruth may not have realized how important and integral her role was; it was an exceeding transformational time for her. Ezekiel Chapters 36 through 39 and Psalms Chapter 112 through Psalms 118 devote a more detailed explanation on the wheat harvest. This harvest represents when the believer is justified by faith. Eventually, Ruth made a complete surrender of her life to Boaz. This represents the sanctified life of the believer. This process is what I call, "sanctifying herself," or "cleansing" or "making holy or pure." Therefore, every child of God or every born-again believer must know the importance of being justified by faith and become overcomers of the world, the flesh and the devil.

I have been spending a great deal of time in these last two chapters suggesting that when you place yourself in the Marvelous Hand of God, marvelous things will happen. The notion that God will only bless you when you are living a "good life" is erroneous. The Bible tells us in Romans that *"while we were still sinners, Christ died for us."* There is no way we can merit God's goodness and grace by our own efforts. God's kindness is eternal and He never changes or goes back on His Word. This act of kindness is illustrated in Ruth Chapter 2 verses 19 through 23. Naomi made a profound and productive statement in verse 19. She said, *"Blessed is the man who took notice of you."* Is it not exciting and exuberating when our Lord takes notice of us? Our Heavenly Father warns us not to worry about the cares of this life. In Matthew Chapter 6, Jesus said that we should not worry about food or drink or even our clothes, because our lives are more important to Him in terms of our worship. So, <u>we should stop worrying and start worshipping</u>! If our

God takes care of the lilies of the field and the birds of the air, what about you and me who are His children? We need to operate by faith and not to worry because worrying is like a cancer that eats away at our spirit and every good cell that inhabits our being. *"But seek first His Kingdom and His Righteousness, and all these things will be given to us as well."* Matthew 6:33. This is exactly what Ruth did, she placed her trust and confidence in the One who will give her a bright future. So, at this juncture of your reading of this book, pause for a moment, rethink and refocus your mind to get it directly in alignment with His will and purpose, just in case it is not there. I would like to expand a little more on verse 19, by giving two biblical illustrations, and then I will also give a couple of present day examples.

Something to ponder on, because it does not matter to God where you are or what you are doing, He will find you. *"Jesus entered Jericho and was passing through. A man was there by the name of Zacchaeus; he was a chief tax collector and was wealthy. He wanted to see who Jesus was, but being a short man he could not, because of the crowd. So he ran ahead and climbed a sycamore – fig tree to see Him, since Jesus was coming that way. When Jesus reached the spot, He looked up and said to him, 'Zacchaeus, come down immediately. I must stay at your house today.' So he came down at once and welcomed him gladly."* Luke 19:1-6. My point in this story is that Zacchaeus was in need of spiritual help. Even though he possessed all of life's treasures which the world looks at to find happiness and joy, he was lacking real peace and joy. Zacchaeus' life was miserable, he was levying high taxes on the poor. I am convinced that he must have heard about Jesus before this encounter and had seen some miracles and even witnessed the conversion of others. In verse 8, Zacchaeus made restitution to everyone from whom he had stolen. This was only possible because of the unconditional love he received from Jesus! Just like Boaz, noticing Ruth and accepting her for who she was, the same way Jesus accepts all sinners the way they are because His blood is efficacious to save and transform them into His likeness and His Righteousness!

My second scriptural illustration of when God notices us is taken from John Chapter 4. Because of the length of the story I would only highlight the important and relevant verses. *"Now He had to go through Samaria. So He came to a town in Samaria called Sychar, near the plot of ground Jacob had given to his son Joseph. Jacob's well was there, and Jesus, tired as He was from the journey, sat down by the well. It was about the sixth hour. When a Samaritan woman came to draw water, Jesus said to her, 'Will you give me a drink?'"* John 4: 4-7. So far, we have seen that Jesus had an encounter with the Samaritan woman. It was certainly not by accident or chance that Jesus was passing through that city. I am pretty sure He could have chosen another time of the day, because that hour of the day seemed to be the very hottest time of the day (sometime around 3pm Eastern Time, in the summer). When it comes to the Lord finding us, despite our situation and condition, He does not care if it is a hail storm, a rain storm or a winter storm. When our God has a blessing for us, like He had for Ruth, He will seek us out to the very end. The story of the Samaritan woman did not end there, because as you continue reading further into Chapter 4 of John, you will discover how Jesus revealed her need of a Savior by revealing the condition of her heart. This beautiful encounter brought about a change of her heart, her mind and definitely a change of her lifestyle. John Chapter 4 and verses 28 and 29 say, *"Then, leaving her water jar, the woman went back to the town and said to the people, 'Come, see a man who told me everything I ever did. Could this be the Christ?'"* She obviously made a complete turn-around with her life, which moments ago was filled with fear, doubts and all kinds of what we may call degrading scenarios. My perspective on both scriptural examples that I just gave is what I call, so frequently in this book, the "Marvelous Hand of God."

As I conclude this chapter and section of the book, I will give you a couple of personal examples of God taking notice of me. In February 2014, as I was getting ready to go on an assignment to preach in Barbados, West Indies, I was also preparing for another business presentation in the United States. Besides my spiritual vocation in the preaching, teaching and edification of God's Holy Word, I am also engaged in secular business. Our family owns a manufacturing facility in Pennsylvania, where we live. We manufacture wall art of different categories. So, getting back to the presentation that I was preparing for, I had a very important meeting with one of my customers whom I would consider as one of my best. As we all sat at the table, the ice was broken and business got on the way immediately. The senior buyer of the company sat directly across from me on the other side of the table. She said, "Before we continue our meeting, I have something to say."

And I quote, "We had a decision to make whether to keep you or the other guys, but we chose you." I must admit, I was a little choked up at first but then my nerves settled very quickly and I was able to finish my presentation with great success! You might be wondering who are the other guys she was talking about. There were a few more competitors in the same business carrying the same categories. Well, I praised the Lord because I knew He was the One Who took notice of me and favored me above the others!

The other incident when my Lord took notice of me was more recent. I was preparing to move my business location due to the fact of the high cost of doing business at that particular location. As you may know, the cost of moving, especially when you have a lot of inventory and heavy machinery, is extremely high. To make this a very short story, the new place to where I was moving the business, the new landlord and I were having a very brief conversation on the move. I asked him if he would have a truck that we could hire to do the move. Standing next to him was a gentleman who I did not know, but he was the landlord's friend and helper. After a couple of minutes talking with each other, they both volunteered to help me with the move. I was so overwhelmed with joy and excitement because, this kind of move would normally cost thousands of dollars, which I did not have at that moment. The landlord asked me to only pay for his gas which amounted to about a hundred dollars and even that he said, "When you get it, you can pay." The other gentleman however, charged a very small amount and then he said to me, "When you get it you can give it to me." I can give you several other examples of how God's Marvelous Hand was and is still in full operation in my life and also that of my family. I want to encourage and exhort you to keep pressing on in your Christian experience. <u>Do not give up, even if you are not seeing anything happening as yet in your life</u>. Jesus will soon break in and when He begins to bless you, be prepared to receive His manifold blessings!

PART IV
RUTH'S PREPARATION PRODUCED GREATNESS: RUTH 3:2-4.

I know of someone whose daughter was diagnosed with breast cancer. For months, she prayed for healing and nothing seemed to be happening. Eventually, the daughter went into remission. I made a comment one day and said to her, "How are dealing with the problem?" She turned to me and said, "Pastor, I never had a problem. It was only a journey and God brought us through successfully." I really liked her response. It was reassuring to know that even though her daughter was afflicted with a disease like cancer, she never wavered in her experience with her Lord, neither did she allow the problem to depress her. Rather, she used it to her advantage and allowed God to work through the circumstance to elevate her to a closer walk with Him. I submit to you that it is extremely important that you keep your eyes fastened on the Lord Jesus Christ and your faith focused on the Cross because whatever journey you may be on, it will become easier for you.

This part of the book that we are entering in is pretty interesting. Some of the terminology that is being used was revealed to me in a non-traditional way. Just do not allow the theology of it dissuade you any way. It is meant to elevate you and empower you for success. You will see that when you follow the direction that God wants to lead you through, the places that He has ordained for you, and the people He has placed in your path, your mind will be filled with His power and presence to take you to another level. Even though Naomi got side-tracked ever so often into the physical and human, Ruth remained forthright and focused! Naomi was giving a very practical suggestion to Ruth when she said, *"Tonight he will be winnowing barley on the threshing floor."* Ruth 3: 2b.

CHAPTER TWELVE
RUTH WAS OBEDIENT TO THE SPIRIT'S CALL

> *When the Lord calls us into greatness, He prepares us by washing us with the water of His pure Word.*

Naomi would sometimes get the right leading of the Spirit to say and do the right things. Does it sound familiar to some of us? Many times, getting into the understanding of how the Spirit operates and launching ourselves forward to operate in the Spirit is slow and filled with reluctance on our part. *"Is not Boaz, with whose servant girls you have been, a kinsman of ours? Tonight he will be winnowing barley on the threshing floor. Wash and perfume yourself, and put on your best clothes. Then go down to the threshing floor, but don't let him know you are there until he has finished eating and drinking. When he lies down, note the place where he is lying. Then go and uncover his feet and lie down. He will tell you what to do."* Ruth 3:2-4. If you really want to see the Holy Spirit working through you, there must be times of you getting close to Him and lying at His feet and waiting for instructions. At this point in Ruth's life, she was risking everything to move forward into greatness, even though she did not realize it. This kind of obedience brings great results for all who obey the Spirit's call like Ruth did.

Peter, who was a very skilled fisherman, was out on the Sea of Galilee. He was fishing one night but caught nothing. Evidently, he was frustrated so he decided to wash his nets and call it a night. Many of us in similar situations may be stopped from realizing our dreams by hindrances or obstacles. Interestingly, Jesus asked Peter to borrow his boat to preach a sermon. I believe that Jesus was trying to teach Peter a lesson on "faith." Jesus could have preached the sermon right on the shore but He wanted to move Peter into a deeper and greater experience! What did Jesus say to Peter that morning? *"Move into the deep with the boat and let the nets down for a catch."* Peter's reluctance, and later, his obedience brought about a miracle. He was stunned and embarrassed because he was a very experienced fisherman and no doubt one of the best in Galilee. That morning, Peter even had to ask for help to lift the net because of the abundance of fish. Peter, realizing his awful condition of living in fear and doubt, confessed them to the Master. <u>Only Jesus can calm every nerve of pain and sorrow and give peace where needed!</u> The big answer for his fear is recorded in Luke. *"Jesus said to Simon, 'Don't be afraid from now on you will catch men.'"* Luke 5:10. The entire account of Peter's miracle can be found in Luke Chapter 5 and verses 1 through 12. The Lord wants us to launch out into the depth of His riches and haul the catch that is awaiting us. Fear, doubt, unbelief and other sins may be holding us back from moving into the Spirit's operation. Everything that happened to Peter in the sense of receiving from the hand of God can happen to us. Peter got great results! Ruth got great results! You can have great results, as well. I can go on to name the many times I got great results in my own life! I can even tell you of many times when my wife got great results from the Lord! This all happens when our lives are yielded to Him and His Holy Spirit is in complete control.

Ruth was asked to wash, perfume herself and put on her best clothes. When the Lord calls us into greatness, He prepares us by washing us with the water of His pure Word. *"Since we have these promises, dear friends, let us purify ourselves from everything that contaminates body and spirit, perfecting holiness out of reverence for God."* 2 Corinthians 7:1. By now, you would realize that Ruth was getting married to Boaz, so she had to present herself pure and clean to him. Since Ruth represents the Christian church, the Lord requires for all His children to be pure and clean. God Himself provided this by the Blood of His own Son and the infallible Word of God. *"Husbands, love your wives, just as Christ loved the church and gave himself up for her to make her holy, cleansing her by the washing with water through the Word, and to present her to Himself as a radiant church, without stain or wrinkle or any other blemish, but holy and blameless."* Ephesians 5:25-27. Ruth's obedience brought her cleansing. She was obedient to Naomi and it produced her cleansing. This is what propelled her into the next chapter of her life. Similarly, for all believers in Christ, we are presented to Him who washes us with the unadulterated Word of God and purifies us with His precious blood which He shed for us on the cross of Calvary.

Ruth was not only cleansed but she was also covered. This is what I call "her obedience brought her a covering." <u>Every child of God needs a covering</u>. We cannot operate on our own and think we are an island to ourselves. We need the covering of the local church that needs the covering of the corporate church. I know of a lot of people who like to work independently. But in times of trouble and difficulty, you will need someone to assist you in dealing with the prevailing problems. Ruth was told by Naomi to perfume herself and to put on her best clothing. Every bride wants to look the best and smell the best at her wedding. After all, it is her big day and best day of her life. The spotlight and focus is on the bride. Similarly, the bride of Christ must look and smell great! *"For we are to God the pleasing aroma of Christ…"* 2 Corinthians 2:15. No stains of the world must be attached to her. The church must be covered with the righteousness of Christ. The devil, the enemy of your precious souls, will try to steal and strip you of the righteousness that you possess in Christ. The devil gives counterfeit clothing and counterfeit perfume. He will say to you, "Do not get married, it is okay to live home with the person (shack up). Try out the person temporarily before you make a permanent commitment." These are all lies and deceit from the enemy who wants you to diminish the purity of the marriage bed and for you to indulge yourselves in sin. He also says to you, "Do not bother making any commitment in your giving, you have too many other expenses to take care of! You do not have to live pure holy and dedicated, just be a 'church-goer!' " If you listen to the enemy's voice and fall into his tricks and schemes, you will eventually end up in the same place where he is, and that is on the way to hell. The devil comes like an angel of light to deceive you, but he also comes like a lion to devour and destroy you! My sincere desire for every born-again believer is for them to listen to the still small voice of the Holy Spirit and do exactly what He requires. No substitutes, period! Obedience, obedience and obedience should be only to the Holy Spirit. I can never over-emphasize the importance of being obedient to the Holy Spirit!

One of my closest friends and brother of the faith, (who is also my brother-in-law), Pastor Paul Richard Watson of Messiah's House in Saint John, Barbados, had a dynamic and refreshing experience with the Holy Ghost in August, 2001. The following is a quote from one of his books (IF IT IS RAINING -- THEN WHY AM I NOT WET?). "On the 23rd August 2001, I encountered the Holy Spirit in a way that has revolutionized both my personal life and public ministry; on that day I received a Baptism of the Holy Spirit and a new anointing for ministry. This Baptism of the Holy Spirit came after twenty-eight (28) years of active and fruitful ministry as a Pastor, Caribbean and District Church Administrator, and as an evangelist throughout the region. It came at a point when I was increasingly disillusioned and dissatisfied with the general state of the church, in the absence of the miraculous and with the powerlessness of the present day ministry. The deep longing of my heart was for something more." What my brother had experienced was fresh fire and fresh power because he was obedient to the Spirit's call and was also operational to the Spirit's counsel. People from all over the island of Barbados came to his church to receive healing and deliverance. His church had experienced "the miraculous" all over them. That church, which was stagnated with a membership of under seventy five people for several decades, began to see supernatural growth. To make his story short, they had to purchase more land to build a larger sanctuary to accommodate the large influx of people. Presently, they have a two-storied sanctuary, seating close to eight hundred (800) people and they are holding two services on Sunday mornings. All this became possible for a man of God who was completely sold out to obeying the Holy Spirit and operating under the Counsel of the Holy Spirit.

Let me give you a promise from the book of Isaiah to show you how the Holy Spirit covers us. "*...to bestow on them a crown of beauty instead of ashes, the oil of gladness instead of mourning, and a garment of praise instead of a spirit of despair. They will be called oaks of righteousness, a planting of the Lord for the display of His splendor.*" Isaiah 61:3. This verse says it all explicitly, revealing what Ruth's life was before she met Boaz. Her life was filled with "ashes, mourning and despair." But her God turned it around in a moment's time. If God wants to work quickly He can do it in a heartbeat. Ruth began to experience, in very great measures, the beautiful Hand of God which brought her such gladness that she never stopped praising Him!

We have to develop seasons of praises to defeat the attack of the enemy! Our lips must be saturated with praises to our Lord. Ruth became an "oak of Righteousness," and the splendor of God was not only all over her, but around everyone she made contact with. Would it not be marvelous if you are an "oak of Righteousness?" <u>No devil in hell will be able to penetrate your life, because you will be solid and firm</u>! Just remember, His splendor is being displayed through you. You will only reflect the righteousness of God as you speak and witness to others. You are the mirror of purity and holiness. The marvelous splendor of God which I call "His Marvelous Hand," is shining through you on a daily basis and everyone who sees it will be in awe. Isaiah went on further to say in verse 10, "*I delight greatly in the Lord, my soul rejoices in my God. For He has clothed me with garments of salvation and arrayed me in a robe of righteousness, as a bridegroom adorns his head like a priest, and as a bride adorns herself with her jewels.*" Isaiah 61:10. This "dressing up" like the grooms and brides was extraordinary looks of magnificence. The groom who is the head of the home must show at all times why he is the head because he is given the authority of leadership. He is the priest of the home.

A bride must also look like a bride. She must at all times be clothed with submission to the groom. The jewels that she is decked up with represent the fruit of the Spirit. This Spirit produces love, kindness, gentleness, peace, joy, longsuffering and patience. There is no condemnation to the one who bears these qualities! Ruth was clothed with these qualities and since Ruth represents the Gentile church then it is imperative that we possess them as well. There are no short cuts, there are no substitutes and certainly there is no working around this. It is a simple requirement in the epistles to be filled with the Spirit of God. Let me clarify also that there is no working our way to heaven by doing good works. But when we are saved and filled with the Spirit of God, then we will want to get busy in His kingdom and always be occupied until the Lord returns. There is a lot to be done in the Kingdom and we all need to be sold out to Christ just like Ruth was sold out to Boaz.

CHAPTER THIRTEEN
RUTH WAS OPERATIONAL TO THE SPIRIT'S COUNSEL

> *There must be a yielding of our spirit to His Spirit in order to comprehend His plan and purpose for our lives.*

Ruth was now getting closer and closer to the "High Calling of God." It is not okay to be just a church-goer, even though when someone goes to church they can receive spiritual help, but God has a bigger and brighter purpose for us. His plans and purposes are beyond our comprehension. There must be a yielding of our spirit to His Spirit in order to comprehend His plan and purpose for our lives.

Ruth was not only satisfied with being obedient to the Spirit's call, but she was ready to operate with the Spirit's counsel. Ruth was ready to act upon all advice given to her and adhere to everything necessary in order to accomplish God's purposes. Are you ready to uncover the spiritual secrets that the Lord has for you? Uncovering those secrets that the Lord has will only be done when your life is in direct correlation with His will and His purpose for which He has ordained for you to carry out. We are in no place to dictate how God should use us in order to accomplish His will through us, even though sometimes we find ourselves trying to do that. Notice in Ruth Chapter 3 and verse 4, Ruth was asked to lie down and uncover Boaz's feet. In other words, we have to fall prostrate at Jesus' feet and learn the secret and art of listening and paying keen attention to the Spirit's counsel.

Do you remember when Jesus was visiting the home of Mary, Martha and Lazarus? Mary took the time to sit, listen and learn at the feet of Jesus, while Martha was more concerned about getting dinner ready. This reminds me of so many folks who miss the opportunity to learn at the feet of Jesus, whether through an Evangelist, or simply through their Pastor. Instead, their schedule is so packed with secular work and the various pressing needs of the day! This is a very old trick of the enemy to occupy your energy elsewhere, rather than learning through the counsel of the Holy Spirit. This is how Ruth responded to the Spirit. " *'I will do whatever you say', Ruth answered. So she went down to the threshing floor and did everything her mother-in-law told her to do. When Boaz had finished eating and drinking and was in good spirits, he went over to lie down at the far end of the grain pile. Ruth approached quietly, uncovered his feet and lay down."* Ruth 3:5-7. There are quite a number of interesting thoughts we will learn from these verses. I will attempt to point them out with the help of the Holy Spirit. Since Ruth was now driving in "high gear," she was in the right place to go in the direction and leadership of the Holy Spirit.

In this day of high technological development, we can be distracted and carried away very easily and may even lose focus with God. Gone are the days when we write a letter, put a stamp and send it through regular mail. Technology is robbing us of directly communicating with our loved ones and associates. If you try to pray and agonize and intercede for lost souls, you are interrupted with the sounds of the cell phone, etc. Facebook, texting, tweeting and Instagram, just to name a few, have all cheated and robbed us of making that direct contact to enjoy a closer relationship with each other. Please do not misunderstand me. I know the value of these modern day technologies, but what I am trying to say is that they have their place in business and society, but we should never allow them to fill the gap of a great relationship with our family and our God! We should not allow them to rob us of the invaluable time that we need to spend with God in the secret place.

The reason our society is out of touch with real spiritual enlightenment and God-given convictions is simply the indulgence of all these substitutes. Ruth's quiet times with Boaz allowed her the privilege and the uncovering of secrets to be made known to her and his desires were much easier for her to understand. I remember as a young preacher, about 30 to 35 years ago, a few of us were spending countless hours of prayer and fasting. As a result, those times with God brought seasons of refreshment spiritually, revival broke out, and many souls were saved. Many were delivered from bad habits that had them bound. We thank the Lord for changing, delivering and transforming the lives of so many people. I personally want to challenge the church to spend more quality and quiet times with the Lord and less time with the things that can so easily rob them of obtaining great results with the Lord. If our Lord Jesus took the time to intercede with His Father, what about you and me? Do you not believe that if we fall prostrate at His feet, we will uncover the deep secrets and revelation that He wants us to share? Psalms Chapter 46 and verse 10 stills rings true today, *"Be still, and know that I am God."*

Elijah experienced victory at Mount Carmel when he defeated the prophets of Baal and the prophets of the groves. Soon after that, Elijah went into depression when Jezebel threatened to kill him, so it sent him spiraling downwards. He lost trust and confidence in the One Who had just helped him to be victorious over the false prophets. I am convinced that Elijah failed to rejuvenate, refuel and recharge his spirit. He failed to spend the same quiet times that had originally given him the strength and stability in the first place. So, God had to remind him as to who is really super powerful, is it Jezebel or is it El Elyon? *"The Lord said, 'Go out and stand on the mountain in the presence of the Lord, for the Lord is about to pass by.' Then a great and powerful wind tore the mountains apart and shattered the rocks before the Lord, but the Lord was not in the wind. After the wind there was an earthquake, but the Lord was not in the earthquake. After the earthquake came a fire, but the Lord was not in the fire. After the fire came a gentle whisper. When Elijah heard it, he pulled his cloak over his face and went out and stood at the mouth of the cave. Then a voice said to him, 'What are you doing here, Elijah?' "* 1 Kings 19:11-13. I have placed quite a reasonable amount of emphasis on being quiet before the Lord, because <u>quietness will produce great results</u>! You are actually putting yourself in the position to hear from Him. Ruth was absolutely quiet at the feet of Boaz and it did produce greatness for her. She got great results! The lesson from Elijah's depression is simple. He failed to recharge himself spiritually! If you are going through a spiritual battle in your life right now, <u>you must recharge and refuel your spiritual life</u>

<u>with the energy and spiritual strength that you will receive only from our Lord Jesus Christ</u>! Take the time to be quiet before Him. I can go on mentioning lots of scriptural examples of men and women who received revelation from the Lord when they utilize some quiet time before God.

I am certainly not advocating that you cannot hear from the Lord by other means like reading His Word, or by the teaching and preaching of His Word or by worshipping Him. However, my emphasis here is based upon Ruth's experience. She got good news when she became quiet before Boaz (who represents Jesus) under the instruction of Naomi her mother-in-law.

I would let you in on my own experience. I was prostrate and quiet before the Lord several times and that is how I received revelation. In fact, writing this book was no ordinary task and by no means simple. The reason I am able to write this book is because the Holy Spirit has given me these thoughts as I penned them. I had never attempted such a feat before, even though I am in ministry for the last 38 years. I had held several different capacities or positions in church administration, but writing a book was never attempted. The point I am making here is that the main reason this book has come into fruition is because the Lord has made it possible. Please do not think of it as something of insignificant value. So, my prayer for you today is that as the Lord opens up your mind and spirit to take you into another level of your ministry (if you are in ministry) or a different level of faith (if you are just a lay person) or even if you have no spiritual inclination. I hope you open up your spiritual ears to hear His voice and pay keen attention as you listen to Him when He speaks.

Ruth chose to go and lie down at the feet of Boaz because that was the appropriate time for her to get her direction and counsel. Great things can take place for us in the "middle of the night." This is the time when everyone wants to rest and take it easy. Sacrifices are something difficult for a lot of people. But, it is important to note that the late hours of the night or the early hours of the morning are considered the best time for us to hear from God. Once again, I am not necessarily advocating that you cannot hear from God at other times. Scriptural example of *"early rising and spending time with God"* is taken from the gospel of Mark. *"Very early in the morning, while it was still dark, Jesus got up, left* the house and went off to a solitary place, where He prayed." Mark 1:35. It is of utmost importance for us to dedicate ourselves to early morning prayer. Even though it may not seem like the most practical time, it can become the most rewarding time in our daily lives. And when we do, we are certain to be overwhelmed with the secrets of heaven.

Another benefit of being operational to the counsel of the Spirit is that we will be crowned with benevolence. " *'Who are you?' he asked. 'I am your servant Ruth,' she said. 'Spread the corner of your garment over me, since you are a kinsman-redeemer.' 'The Lord bless you, my daughter', he replied."* Ruth 3:9-10a. Ruth's request was to enjoy just a piece of His covering. God's grace is immeasurable. All we need is just a portion to cover us. Ruth recognized that if she could only get a portion of his covering, she would be blessed forever. In the gospel of Luke Chapter 8, we read the account of the woman who was bleeding for twelve years. She went and touched the border of Jesus' garment and she received her healing. She just wanted to touch a small part of Him because she knew that a miracle would take place for her. It does not take much for God to bless you. Ruth made herself available to the counsel of the Holy Spirit and blessings followed her all the way.

Another benefit or effect of the Holy Spirit upon our lives is that the goodness of the Lord leads us all the time. Even when you feel like you are alone and helpless, just trust Him because He is there with you. Isaiah gives two very important nuggets of inspiration. *"Then will all your people be righteous and they will possess the land forever. They are the shoot I have planted, the work of my hands, for the display of my splendor."* Isaiah 60:21. In other words, when God's "Marvelous Hand" is upon us, He will display His awesome splendor. This is what I call "God's goodness leading us." Isaiah went on to strengthen his point; *"Instead of their shame my people will receive a double portion, and instead of disgrace they will rejoice in their inheritance; and so they will inherit a double portion in their land, and everlasting joy will be theirs."* Isaiah 61:7. This is a marvelous promise of God's leadership in every area of our lives. Ruth had no more shame, disgrace or disappointment following her. She was full of the Grace of God and therefore God's leadership was upon her in great measure.

Every born-again believer in the new covenant will be allotted a double portion of blessing. Just imagine your life before conversion; a mess, full of shame and disgrace, but now full of the abundant goodness of God. God's promise to us, who are His children, is to enjoy everlasting joy, not a temporary one. A life that was once in darkness and despondency will now have the glorious light of the gospel shining through and through!

The goodness of the Lord does not only lead us but also the goodness of the Lord leans on us. People's burdens and problems may press us and take us downwards. So, if we are not strong spiritually, their burdens can become a dead weight to carry. Instead, they need to be lifted up and counselled by the mighty hand of God. When God leans on us, He is leaning love that is unstoppable, unchangeable, unshakeable and joy that is unspeakable, which the scripture says is "full of His glory." He sheds increasing faith that is unsinkable and a sound mind that is stable. God leans love, compassion and all good things that He is desirous for us to have. *"Who redeems your life from the pit and crowns you with love and compassion, who satisfies your desires with good things so that your youth is renewed liked the eagle's."* Psalms 103:4-5. This scripture is such a classic example of God leaning on us with every good thing that we need. *"Satisfy us early in the morning with your unfailing love, that we may sing for joy and be glad all our days."* Psalms 90:14. Moses had an extraordinary experience with the Lord during the time when God delivered the Israelites from the hand of Pharaoh while they were in Egypt. God also extended His unfailing love and grace toward the Israelites while they were wandering through the wilderness. It was an amazing time for the Israelites as God provided each day. He met all their physical needs and also protected them from the hands of the enemies. These scriptural illustrations that I just gave is what I call "God leaning His unfailing and merciful Hand upon us <u>even when we do not deserve it</u>."

To complete this chapter, I have to give you another characteristic of Ruth. Ruth's character was befitting or unblemished. In other words, she lived a pure life. Ruth was not contaminated by the effects of the environment. <u>She drew every line that had to be drawn to maintain her purity and stability</u>! Many young ladies at her age, and being a widow, would have been tempted to run after the fleshly desires and the worldly affairs. But this young lady displayed a completely different attitude.

"*And now, my daughter, don't be afraid. I will do for you all you asked. All my fellow townsmen know that you are a woman of noble character.*" Ruth 3:11. Ruth's unblemished record opened the eyes of Boaz. He knew from the very inception when he met her that she was different from the other girls. God accepts us just as we are, but when He changes us and sanctifies us through and through, He will keep us pure and holy. God will preserve our character in the midst of this crooked and debased society in which we live. It really does not matter when people try to debase or belittle you, because they will. I want to assure you that your God will preserve and protect you from the evils of the day.

The apostle Paul gave us a very compelling statement of those who are in Christ. "*So that you may become blameless and pure, children of God without fault in a crooked and depraved generation, in which you shine like stars in the universe...*" Philippians 2:15. This is an absolute and beautiful statement that the Apostle Paul gives to describe the child of God who is marked with purity and holiness all over him or her. He describes all born-again Christians like stars shining in the universe. This tells me that we who are identifying ourselves as followers of Christ must be extremely careful how we carry ourselves in this world. There is a great impact or influence that is being reflected off of us in this depraved and sin-sick world. We are a priceless people in this world today and the sad fact is many of us are not shining in the way we should. There needs to be more togetherness and cooperation among believers and less bickering and fault-finding.

CHAPTER FOURTEEN
RUTH WAS OVERWHELMED BY THE SPIRIT'S COMFORT

> *When blessings from the Lord begin to follow us, they may come in large numbers. God will bring back an abundance of "double for your trouble." Your future will be brighter, bigger and bountiful.*

The secret to an abundant and satisfied life is to live a deep life of humility. We must be humble and remain humble at all times. Ruth lived a humble and pure life and she reaped a harvest. I will attempt to explore Ruth Chapter 3 and verse 15. There is great significance when it comes to numbers that are mentioned in the Holy Scriptures. It is very intriguing when it comes to certain numbers. *"He also said, 'Bring me the shawl you are wearing and hold it out.' When she did so, he poured into it six measures of barley and put it on her. Then he went back to town."* Ruth 3:15.

The shawl is an oblong piece of cloth that covers the head and shoulders. Most Jewish men and women used a shawl to pray. These shawls are also highlighted with many scriptures. Whether Ruth's shawl was a prayer cloth or just a covering for her head is not known. What is important to note is that Ruth's shawl was used to receive the blessing that Boaz had given her. "Six measures of barley is the same as six seahs. A seah contained about two and a half gallons. So six measures must be a pretty heavy load for a woman to lift" (Jamieson Fausset- Brown Bible commentary). Gill's exposition of this is "proof of Boaz's kindness to Ruth and that she was acceptable to him." Gill went on to interpret six blessings that shall be bestowed on her, as the spirit of wisdom, the spirit of understanding, the spirit of counsel, the spirit of power, the spirit of knowledge and the spirit of the fear of the Lord," as mentioned in Isaiah Chapter 11 and verse 2. The interpretations may not be accurate from any of the commentators, but what is well known to us is that she was blessed beyond her comprehension and imagination.

Fifteen gallons of barley was a very large amount for one person. The most important information that I would like to share with you in regards to the reception of the fifteen gallons of barley is the amount of blessings that Ruth received. When blessings from the Lord begin to follow us and fall on us they may come in large numbers. Remember, barley harvest represents that you are an overcomer. Evidently, Ruth was overcoming her bankruptcy. You must consider the fact that when Ruth first came to Bethlehem, she had no job, no money, and no one knew her, except Naomi. Now, as you may remember, Naomi was filled with bitterness and fear. So Ruth really and truly had nothing to work with but zero dollars. What I do know is the fact that this young lady was very determined to make it work for her. She was willing to make the necessary changes in her life in order to gain access to heaven's treasure. Depression, deterrence, despondency and distraction were not in her vocabulary. The responses toward difficult and dangerous times can either set us back or they can shape our destiny. This young lady was absolutely amazing. She held out her shawl and it was filled to capacity, more than she could use. She had enough to spare and to share. Are you holding out your shawl to receive from the hands of the Lord?

This experience of holding out the shawl is what I deem to be the overflow of the Spirit. I may take a lot of heat theologically for this interpretation, but like as I said before, a lot of this writing is pure revelation from the Lord. Lots of folks are holding back on receiving the infilling of the Holy Spirit. They need to recognize the move of God today and be ready to hold that shawl out and receive the abundance of the over flow of the Holy Spirit in these last days in which we live. This overflow of God upon us will certainly take us to the next level in our walk with God.

The devil thinks he has victory over you because of the losses you suffer. You need to be brave and bold and be ready to receive because your God will bring back an abundance of "double for your trouble." Your future will be brighter, bigger and bountiful. I say this with much confidence. I have been knocked down numerous times by the enemy. They were very big blows, but every time I rose up and I am now stronger and wiser, because it was a learning curve. So, the devil is a big loser. He does not realize he is dealing with a veteran in God's kingdom and these last 38 years have been filled with lots of spiritual blessings. Even though the challenges were severe and heart-wrenching at times during my Christian journey, the blessings from the Lord far outweigh them all by a thousand percent. The fact that I am breathing and able to teach, preach, encourage, exhort and write this book is ample evidence of God's amazing love and God's Marvelous Hand in full operation.

Moses was on a "spiritual high" when he declared, *"May your deeds be shown to your servants, your splendor to their children."* Psalms 90:16. Moses experienced God's care and comfort from the time of his birth, floating in the Nile River up through the palace of Pharaoh, through the Exodus and finally through the wilderness. Moses was asking God not to only bless him but also to bless his posterity. Ruth fell into this category of blessing and she received it at the right time. Nothing with God is out of time and focus. Everything with God is ordained with purpose and clarity. Negativity and failings may come your way, but remember that the Lord's splendor is about to fall on you and shine through you. You are in your Father's hand and He has your rewards waiting for you to inherit.

Moses went on further to say, *"May the favor of the Lord our God rest upon us; establish the work of our hands for us - Yes, establish the work of our hands."* Psalms 90:17. Moses was a man of God who knew exactly what it meant to have God's favor upon his life. What were the odds for a little Hebrew baby boy floating in the Nile River in Egypt and the Egyptian soldier missing him? When God's favor is upon you He even uses the unbeliever to show you favor. In Moses's case, God used Pharaoh's daughter to protect Moses. I trust you are now getting a full idea and clearer understanding of what God's favor is and what it means to have God establishing the work of our hands.

Let me take you back to the mid 1970's. A close friend of mine, Mahase Singh and I, started a Sunday School in a small country village. In those days, we used to call it "the bottom-house church." In Guyana, SA, the poor people built their houses on wooden columns while the affluent people built their houses on concrete columns. To paraphrase my story, we were holding Sunday School classes under the house. There was also a cult holding services in another house which was not very far from us. Several times, these cultists threatened us to move out of the area. God's "Marvelous Hand" of favor was upon us and we managed to successfully stand our ground. Subsequently, the Lord opened up the door for us to have adult services there as well. So, we did not have Sunday School classes only, but we started adult services because we persevered and did not allow the threats to dampen or destroy our vision. Today, that church still exists but has moved to a different location.

I want to exhort and encourage you to remain faithful to your calling even if at this juncture you are facing persecution or circumstances beyond your control. God's favor is about to be shown in your direction and He will establish the work of your hands. The prophet Habakkuk speaks about the favor of God this way, *"Lord, I have heard of your fame; I stand in awe of your deeds, O Lord. Renew them in our day, in our time make them known…"* Habakkuk 3:2. This was a sincere prayer of the man of God who saw darkness and violence on every hand during his time of ministry. So, he cried out for God to do something about the situation. He said that he realized the awesomeness and power of God. He realized God did it in the past, but now they were not seeing God's hand moving because they were not having revival. Do you feel sometimes like the prophet Habakkuk? Then I would suggest that we begin to cry out to God and ask Him to move again among us because He wants to do it.

God is not satisfied with dry worship and worldly living. I am talking about being overwhelmed with the care and comfort of the Holy Spirit. I sincerely pray that the Lord will grant us a revelation of our lost condition and that we will seek Him earnestly and then we will experience Him in His fullness. We are in dire need of the Holy Spirit in and around our churches to get rid of selfishness and pride that are so prevalent. We also need the Holy Spirit among our families to bring unity and harmony. The devil is working overtime to destroy and divide families, marriages and even churches. Some of us are naming the name of Christ and taking it easy in our ministry while back-biting and stabbing one another prevails. Sadly, there is a spirit of complacency in some of our churches. We will eventually destroy each other if these carnal traits are found among us. It is time to get our shawls open wide so that we can receive the abundant care of the Spirit.

Here are three thoughts that I gleaned from Habakkuk Chapter 3 and verse 2.

(i) The works of God are manifested. This is what the prophet was praying for, and certainly all of us, whether layman or ministerial, we should pray the same earnest prayer.

(ii) The wisdom of God is displayed. If there were ever a time when we all need the wisdom of God in this degenerate society where some people cannot differentiate between good and evil, right and wrong, sin and righteousness, it is now. God's wisdom needs to be displayed by every born-again Christian to help them in their decision-making.

(iii) The will of God is renewed daily. So many of us get caught in the trap of not renewing ourselves before the Lord daily. This is the reason we get tangled up with the wrong ideas. When I say, "renewed daily," I do not mean we have to confess our sins daily, but we need to make that commitment with the Lord. We need a strong reminder each day that we are His and He is ours.

Jesus said, *"I have much more to say to you, more than you can now bear. But when He, the Spirit of Truth, comes, He will guide you into all truth. He will not speak on His own; He will speak only what He hears, and He will tell you what is yet to come. He will bring glory to Me by taking from what is Mine and making it known to you."* John 16:12-14. In other words, the Spirit of God will guide us daily into the truth of His inspired Word and we will get our "rhema" word through obedience to Him. As we study and meditate on God's Word daily, He gives us the wisdom that we need in our daily Christian walk. The ultimate advantage for every born-again believer is to seek the infilling of the Holy Spirit. The Holy

Spirit is our Comforter Who gives us the strength we need to deal with the uncertainties that may occasionally come along our path.

All of the apostles were among the believers who sought and received the Baptism of the Holy Ghost. It was commanded by our Lord Himself when He said, "Wait for the Promise of the Father." Again He said, *"But you will receive power when the Holy Spirit comes on you, and you will be my witnesses in Jerusalem, and in all Judea and Samaria, and to the ends of the earth."* Acts 1:8. Much time has been spent on this chapter, explaining the importance of being filled with the Holy Spirit. Ruth's experience was a type of the infilling of the Holy Spirit and she represents the church which needs the infilling of the Holy Spirit as well. If you are not filled, I submit to you that you need to seek Him out until you are filled. You can prepare yourself for greatness. We will be overwhelmed with His presence only when the Holy Spirit fills us. This cannot be done out of a prideful heart but a humble heart because God debases a prideful heart but he exalts a humble heart. As you seek Him earnestly, He will help you to rid yourself of all the hindrances and fleshly appetites. God has no problem filling you with His power. This power will help you live above sin and reproach and will give you the authority to trample on the schemes of the enemy.

PART V
RUTH EXTENDED HER LEGACY: RUTH 3:18 – 4:22.

Ruth started out on what seemed to be a dark, despondent and dismal relationship. However, God soon turned it around for her, making it a very deliberate, delightful and durable relationship. Many times, it really does not matter how you start, what really matters most is how you finish! You can have a shaky and doubtful start, but if you keep in the right direction you will finish strong.

In the 2014 National Football Conference, the Arizona Cardinals started the season with great success. In the first ten games they were nine wins and one loss. Sports analysts were selecting them to finish first in their conference. But soon after, things began to unravel and they lost focus and direction. As a result, they could not maintain the momentum that they had at the beginning. So, in the last six games of the regular season, they had one win and five losses, ending the season at ten wins and six losses. What was more devastating was the fact that they had lost their first playoff game to a much "inferior" team, the Carolina Panthers, which ended the season with a record of eight wins and seven losses and one draw. My point is that as we travel along this Christian pathway, obstacles will come. At the very onset of our Christian walk, the enemy will attack and will discourage us in order to get us to turn back. But, we must remain focused and stay on our winning ways.

The Arizona Cardinals apparently changed their game plan and that resulted in losses for them. We must stay the course and ride every wave that comes to delay and distract us. Sometimes, they may even throw us off-course, but we must remember the ways of the Lord and use the sword of the Spirit and the Word of the Lord to guide us through the channel that we need to take. It takes faith and trust in Him to take us through. The book of the Epistle of James says, *"God gives wisdom liberally to all who ask."* Ruth was definitely on course to finish strong because her heart was set and her mind made up, to do one and only one thing, that is, to become the person that God wanted her to be. The worldly attractions and allurements had no effect on her, whether present or future. Every word of discouragement that she had heard from Naomi obviously did not penetrate or hurt her. That was one of the main reasons she left such a legacy. We all need to keep moving forward and not get side-tracked and put ourselves into a backward motion. Instead, we have to press forward and move to the goal and the mark of "The High calling of God." The first quality that Ruth possessed to enhance her or propel her into this great legacy was patience.

CHAPTER FIFTEEN
RUTH EXERCISED PATIENCE

> *Patience is a very sweet quality, but can be a very painful experience. Our rewards are always bigger than our troubles as we continue to exercise patience through the help of the Holy Spirit.*

"Then Naomi said, 'Wait, my daughter, until you find out what happens. For the man will not rest until the matter is settled today.'" Ruth 3:18. Patience is a very sweet quality that every one of us needs to possess. However, it can be a very painful experience because as Romans Chapter 5 and verse 3 says, *"...tribulation works patience."* We are living in a day and age when everything seems to be on the fast track. You know the saying, "live fast and die young." The restaurants are filled every day with people because many are finding it difficult to home-cook their food. Restaurants are packed mainly on the weekends, including certain holidays and special occasions. Gone are the days when families got together and sat down to enjoy a good old-fashioned homemade dinner, except on certain occasions like Thanksgiving and Christmas. Microwave food is substituted for a good home-cooked meal. When you sit to have fellowship together and enjoy your meal at home, texting, emailing, tweeting, instagramming, etc., have been stealing the precious time of fellowship and communion. Now, please do not misinterpret my motives. Nothing is wrong with using the technological devices that I have just mentioned to accomplish your goals and assignments, if used in the correct manner. These new technologies can be a great asset to society and used as a great advantage to us, if channeled accurately. We

must never allow these machines and devices to substitute for a good fellowship, especially our invaluable moments with our Lord and Savior, Jesus Christ.

When we really want to see impatience at its best, check out a traffic jam that can be miles long. Drivers cut off others which can sometimes create road-rage, havoc and accidents. If you want to witness impatience at its highest level, try getting into a subway car during peak hours in New York City! Impatience is prevalent also when flights are delayed for hours. Impatience is displayed at sports, especially when the game is on the line. At schools, we have a great deal of impatience among students. When the entire debacle is over, it is then everyone who was involved looks back and says, "How stupid was that!" You also hear other remarks like, "I should have known better!" These are only a few that I am mentioning. I strongly suggest that if you are going to be successful with the Lord Jesus and be a worker in the Kingdom, you will have to exercise patience.

Ruth evidently showed a great deal of patience and that is why she was able to overcome all obstacles. She learned the art because she took part in the barley harvest, which means "overcomers." When we are filled with the Spirit of God, we will surely possess patience. After all, patience is the fruit of the Spirit. So, it is impossible to say you are filled with the Spirit of God and lack patience. Patience will be a part of your lifestyle.

Ruth had done everything right since she came to Bethlehem with Naomi her mother-in-law. Her journey was not always perfect and I am pretty sure there were lots of bottlenecks along the way. But, those hindrances and obstacles only came her way to make her a much stronger person. That is one of the main reasons that, at this point, Ruth could have exercised the kind of patience that she was exercising. After spending so many years with Ruth, Naomi began to come to grips with the reality that something special was in this young lady and she had what it takes to successfully complete this journey. Before we can really have patience, we must go through trouble. Trouble will either make us or break us. I am confident that when you go through trouble, and you have the Lord as your leader, you will be victorious! You will either be made whole when trouble comes or you will be torn apart. You will see very shortly how Ruth's patience paid off with large dividends, and remember, if you remain strong and stable in your trouble you will also gain great dividends.

As I have been saying to you in previous chapters, my life along with that of my family's was filled with lots of troubles, but our God has always rewarded us with His goodness. Our rewards are always bigger than our troubles as we continue to exercise patience through the help of the Holy Spirit. Ruth was advised by Naomi to wait and she did not let that advice fall by the wayside, but rather she acted upon it and was rewarded in a very positive manner. She waited to see that the matter would be settled for her "today," not tomorrow or next week or a year later, but "today." When we fully surrender to the Lord, there is no telling what great blessings He has in store for us. However, we will have to exercise patience. There is always a time fixed with God when it comes to Him answering our prayers and requests. It may seem like God is far away and you are not hearing from Him, but please exercise the patience that is needed and the answer will be revealed sooner than you may think. I am not asking you to do something that I did not do, because I had to show patience during my times of suffering, and God always showed up at the right time.

Ruth was about to receive the greatest turn around in her life. What she received was nothing she expected. You see, our God has a way of replenishing our needs in a greater way than what it was before. Ruth was an unknown pagan girl whom the Lord transformed by His power and all she received time and time again was the love and grace of God. If you have not begun to see any reward as yet in your Christian walk, do not lose heart or do not be discouraged. The light at the end of the tunnel is about to shine your way. Keep your faith and hope strong and keep holding on to the Word of His Power and the rewards will come. All it will take is a "little cloud the size of a man's hand." "*Elijah sent out his servant several times before he finally saw the cloud. It was the seventh time that the servant saw the cloud which was the size of a man's hand.*" I Kings 18:44. This is God's perfect number. The cloud appeared on the seventh time that the servant went out. My point is, it will take patience on our part to see the Marvelous Hand of God. Make no mistake, God answers the request and prayer at an appointed time which He fixes. We cannot fix the times for eternal events, we need our Eternal God and Father to do His work. All we need to do is be patient and wait on Him for the right time.

The prophet Isaiah gave us a very good example of waiting as well the benefits. *"But those who hope in the Lord will renew their strength. They will soar on wings like eagles; they will run and not grow weary, they will walk and not faint."* Isaiah 40:31. When you are feeling weak, lonely, and depleted, seek the face of the Lord to renew your strength. When your strength is renewed by the Lord, He will make you feel like you are soaring high like eagles. In other words, your problems will be below you and you will be above them! You will be running and not getting tired, walking and not fainting. Basically, all the everyday situations that you will face will not be a bother but they all will pass by like nothing has happened. Your spiritual arms and legs will be strengthened and will enable you to be overcomers.

Patience involves a process. God works through our disappointments and sorrows. He may not take them away from us, but He certainly will always make a way for us to cast out the uneasy feeling of fear that may come as a result of our sorrows. God made a way for Ruth as she endured her trials which may have seemed unsurmountable. Processes are something that many Christians try to avoid, especially when they are painful and difficult to bear. But let me assure you that our Lord will not leave us stranded to go through our sorrows alone. He will send the Comforter to strengthen and sustain us during those dark moments that may seem never-ending.

May I elaborate a little on the process that Jesus had to go through in order for Him to accomplish the task for which He was sent to accomplish? Our Lord and Savior, Jesus Christ, faced the toughest process that any human being could ever think or imagine. The Bible tells us, *"He withdrew about a stone's throw beyond them, knelt down and prayed…, 'Father, if You are willing, take this cup from Me; yet not My will, but Yours be done.' An angel from heaven appeared to Him and strengthened Him. And being in anguish, He prayed more earnestly, and His sweat was like drops of blood falling to the ground."* Luke 22:41-44. This event started the final process that Jesus took for the sins of mankind. As you could imagine, it was not an easy process by any stretch of the imagination. Think about Him praying with such intensity and fervor, the effect it created was like blood falling off from Him as He was sweating. This was truly an agonizing experience, causing an angel from heaven to come to His aid to give Him the strength that He needed. This process continued with His unlawful arrest in Gethsemane, His illegal trials between Pilate and the Sanhedrin court, and finally, the cruel beatings and unmerciful torture that He endured after which He was taken up to Calvary where He was crucified between two criminals. This is what I call an extreme, dire process but He endured it with patience. I exhort you today, as you go through your sufferings and what you may call your painful tragedies, be reminded that your Lord went through a much more difficult process. The main thing that upheld Him was the fact that He exercised patience. Therefore, you must endure your process in trials by exercising the same patience.

The process that we have to go through will involve a risk. Let me remind you that when Moses's mother, Jochebed, put him in a basket to float him in the Nile River while Moses's sister looked on; they took a risk. They were not sure what would have happened to him. All they did was took the risk and left the rest up to God. What exactly was the risk that they took? Moses's life was in danger because Pharaoh wanted him dead and so, if they put him in a basket, who knows if one of the aristocrats of Egypt would have mercy on him and spare his life. As it turned out, Pharaoh's daughter saw him, and God changed her heart whereby she showed compassion and she took Moses and kept him as her son. The plan and process was very risky, but well rewarded. There is a song that says, "He never promised us a victory without fighting, He said help would always come on time."

"At this, the kinsman-redeemer said, '...then I cannot redeem it because I might endanger my own estate. You redeem it yourself. I cannot do it.'" Ruth 4:6. What kind of a redeemer would say something like that? Obviously, the one who does not have a committed heart and caring love. His eyes were swaying towards the flesh and he failed to conquer the flesh through the spirit. This man who was supposed to be the rightful redeemer, I have likened him to Adam who failed in his assignment to be the kind of husband and leader of his family. He obviously failed because he did not want to take the risk of protecting his wife. As a result, Adam lost his authority to conquer the flesh and therefore enabled the enemy to make in-roads very easily. When the

three Hebrew boys refused to bow down before the golden image that was made by Nebuchadnezzar, they took a serious risk. The Bible gives us the following account in the book of Daniel. *"If we are thrown into the blazing furnace, the God we serve is able to save us from it, and He will rescue us from your hand, O King. But even if He does not, we want you to know, O king, that we will not serve your gods or worship the image of gold you have set up."* Daniel 3:17-18. This entire process involved a risk. Our walk with Jesus is definitely not "a walk in the park."

"For the Lord God is a sun and shield; the Lord bestows favor and honor; no good thing does He withhold from those whose walk is blameless. O Lord Almighty, blessed is the man who trusts in you." Psalms 84:11-12. The following statements are what I gleaned from these two verses.

(i) The Lord is a light that shines in the dark. When you feel like you are being overshadowed with darkness, just remember to apply Psalms Chapter 84 and remind yourself that the light of His presence is brighter than the darkness that came upon you. So, you need not to grope and fear in the dark because the light of Jesus is all over you.

(ii) The Lord is not only a light that shines in the dark but He is a defense that devours the enemy. Here again, when you feel like you have been trampled on by the enemy and you are in a very dangerous state and helpless situation, your God is right there to defend you and take you up in His wide arms of protection. The devil's arrows of doubt, discouragement and failure would not penetrate you because Jesus is your defense. Or preferably, you can say He is your shield. The enemy has many imps that he sends to overcome your spirit. It does not matter how much they try, they all will fail because you are surrounded by God's Presence. So, it is time to rise up and take back what the devil has stolen from you! You have someone on your side who is much stronger than the devil. The word of God tells us, *"...the One Who is in you is greater than the one who is in the world."* I John 4:4b. Who would you rather trust with your life? The devil who has been crippled and crushed or the Lord who is victorious over the flesh, the devil and the world?

(iii) The Lord is not only a light that shines and a defense that devours the enemy, but He sheds favor and honor on the believers. Psalms Chapter 84 and verse 11b says, "*He bestows favor and honor.*" Our Lord gives us favor and honor even when we do not deserve them. No plan or scheme of the enemy can prevent the blessings of the Lord. Nothing could have kept Ruth back from extending her legacy. She was fully prepared. Obviously, the patience that she acquired over the years came through her perseverance and her commitment. I want to encourage you to stay in the focus lane and never allow the enemy to drown your mind in the filth of this world which is heading downward further and further out of the will of God. Your heavenly Father bestows favor and honor on you. That means you are blessed beyond human comprehension. What may seem difficult in the eyes of the world is only a possibility for you because His favor is upon you. Jesus said, "*…everything is possible for him who believes.*" Mark 9:23b.

We are not only blessed with favor, we are also blessed with honor. What does it mean to be honored? The enemy will try his best to talk down to us and belittle us, but remember, you are God's chosen vessel and He will lift you up and honor you. In the book of Esther, the story is told of the wicked man Haman who tried to influence king Xerxes to annihilate the Jews by trying to get rid of Mordecai. Haman even got some others involved in the plot to hang Mordecai. But God intervened in the matter and used Queen Esther to go before the King and she pleaded for the life of Mordecai and the Jews. The same gallows that was prepared by Haman to hang Mordecai was in return used to hang Haman. My point is, through all the debacles, God turned the situation around and honored Mordecai instead. We all can have the blessings of the Lord overtake us but our lives will have to be dedicated and committed to Him and His work. This is all possible when we exercise patience like Ruth did and God will work everything out in His timetable. Never rush God. We have to possess the quality of patience like Ruth did and the benefits and rewards will chase after us.

CHAPTER SIXTEEN
BOAZ EXECUTED THE POWER OF ATTORNEY

> *In our desperate and destitute condition, our Lord Jesus offers the deepest sympathy, the most loving care and the strongest devotion.*

"Then Boaz announced to the elders and all the people. 'Today you are witnesses that I have bought from Naomi all the property of Elimelech, Kilion and Mahlon. I have also acquired Ruth the Moabitess, Mahlon's widow, as my wife, in order to maintain the name of the dead with his property, so that his name will not disappear from among his family or from the town records. Today you are witnesses!'" Ruth 4: 9-10. These two verses are profoundly stated and have great spiritual significance. This is a perfect love story that brought two different people from different backgrounds and training together as one unit. One of them was Ruth who was a foreigner and she was not quite sure what her future would entail. The other was Boaz who knew exactly what he was up to and knew what he wanted to do. As we can see, his love for Ruth went far beyond the physical. As a matter of fact, this man Boaz took all the risks in the world to make this girl, who did not have much of a future, his bride.

The beautiful and amazing lesson that we all have learned from this exceptional love affair is very clear. There were no fears and doubts attached. Boaz took the full responsibility to purchase all the rights pertaining and belonging to Ruth. Also, do not be mistaken, this was a very costly and weighty package for him. Evidently, the size of her problem did not matter much to Boaz. He had a sense of peace, no matter what the cost was. The choice was solely Boaz's decision to purchase Ruth with everything that she possessed. Boaz had the entire eldership of the town to witness this selfless and strange marriage. No one coerced Boaz to marry her. He saw the great potential that she had and he saw someone who was precious and someone who could catapult others into greatness as well.

So, what is the spiritual and marvelous connection and what is the significance? Just as Boaz took complete ownership of Ruth with all her baggage and belongings, the same way Jesus took over the responsibility and ownership to save lost mankind. Jesus said, *"For the Son of Man came to seek and to save what was lost."* Luke 19:10. What exactly was lost? The fellowship, the communion, the love, the peace, the joy, the protection, the provision, and the beautiful and serene atmosphere were all lost. The real contentment of knowing and believing that everything is well was stolen by the enemy. Adam and Eve listened to the lies of the enemy of their souls and transgressed against God. For centuries, mankind had to make all kinds of blood sacrifices to atone for their sins but when the "fullness of time" came, God sent His Son in the person of Jesus Christ and made atonement for the sins of fallen mankind. Our Jesus brought back peace, love, joy, life, and life with all of its abundance. What was a lost people, became legal citizens through our Lord and Savior, Jesus Christ.

We were all depraved and condemned to die. We were a very lost people but now we are legal citizens of heaven. Even though we did not deserve to abide in His presence, Jesus still made it all possible. This is what I call "God's Amazing Grace" and this is what Ruth enjoyed through Boaz. Ruth was in the right place at the right time. As stated earlier, Ruth represents the Gentile church. In our desperate and destitute condition, our Lord Jesus offers the deepest sympathy, the most loving care and the strongest devotion. He is always there to protect us from every dart that the enemy throws and His presence is there even though sometimes we may not feel it. We do have to trust Him by faith. We have to be confident in Him and believe Him that He will do what He says. Nothing happens by chance in God's kingdom. Everything was planned before the foundation of the world. God has a divine plan and determined purpose for every one of His children. Let me suggest, that even though Ruth was a Moabitess and may have thought at first that there was no hope, she knew what Bethlehem represented and she knew the treasures that were ahead. So, she did not allow negative words and negative feelings to deprive her of real success. I want to also suggest that if you keep prodding along and keep believing in the "Marvelous Hand of God," you will see that a way is already made for you through our Lord Jesus Christ. We just need to hold on to His unchanging hand as we continue on this journey of faith.

As I was saying, just as Boaz executed the power of attorney to purchase Ruth with all her baggage and belongings, our Lord Jesus executed a similar power of attorney to purchase our lives and reconcile us back to His Father. Communion with our Father was lost in the Garden of Eden through the disobedience of Adam and Eve. So, the redemption plan that was executed by Jesus included all our past sins, our present sins and if we commit future sins. God's hands are marvelous and mysterious. You may begin to see some strange things happening in your life, and when they do happen, do not be appalled or dismayed, God's "Marvelous Hand" is at work.

The Apostle Paul made it clear to the church at Galatia that our redemption, like Ruth's, was orchestrated by our Heavenly Father. *"But when the time had fully come, God sent His Son, born of a woman, born under law, to redeem those under law, that we might receive the full rights of sons. Because you are sons, God sent the Spirit of His Son into our hearts, the Spirit who calls out, 'Abba, Father.' So you are no longer a slave, but a son; and since you are a son, God has made you also an heir."* Galatians 4:4-7. From these Scriptures, you could see that it was orchestrated and planned by our Heavenly Father. Nothing was by accident, nothing was a guess-plan, not even luck as some may believe. This was the right moment. It was the precise and accurate timing of the triune God-Head. We are now children of God. We have been made legal citizens of heaven. We are not illegal people or aliens in a foreign country. We have been bought with the precious blood of Jesus and have been placed under the full custody of our Heavenly Father. We have the full rights and privileges of being called sons and not slaves anymore. We are heirs and joint-heirs in the kingdom of God!

Before I make mention of another Scripture that would shed some light on the fact that we are heirs in the kingdom, I would like to reiterate why Ruth was given full rights and privileges in Boaz's estate. You see, Ruth was obedient to the Spirit and exercised total patience. While some may advocate that you do not really need to be obedient and live pure to earn a place in the kingdom, the Word of God made it very clear. *"Make every effort to live in peace with all men and to be holy; without holiness no one will see the Lord."* Hebrews 12:14. *"May God himself, the God of peace, sanctify you through and through. May your whole spirit, soul and body be kept blameless at the coming of our Lord Jesus Christ."* I Thessalonians 5:23. The Bible tells us emphatically that no sin will enter heaven. So, what's the point? Even though Christ died for us and paid the penalty for sin, we must repent and live godly and pure in this present world in order to make it to heaven.

I now close this chapter strongly by referring to another Scripture of utmost importance. *"And hope does not disappoint us, because God has poured out His love into our hearts by the Holy Spirit, whom He has given us."* Romans 5:5. Ruth's perseverance and hope did not disappoint her. We could see all the love that was poured into her from Boaz. Similarly, the Holy Spirit is our Comforter and abiding peace. Therefore, we need not to be afraid or be depressed over any matter of concern. *"For you did not receive a spirit that makes you again to fear, but you received the Spirit of son-ship. And by Him we cry, 'Abba, Father.' The Spirit Himself testifies with our spirit that we are God's children. Now if we are children, then we are heirs - heirs of God and co-heirs with Christ, if indeed we share in His sufferings in order that we may also share in His Glory."* Romans 8:15-17. When you repent of your sins, you become a child of God. However, the time will come when you will suffer in this life as a believer and the rewards will be astounding. You will automatically share in His glory. So, even if you never acquire much in this present life, the time will come when you will share in His glory and that will be more than enough to ask for. It is very clear from these verses in Romans Chapter 8 that the sufferings will present itself first before the glory is experienced.

Before Christ perfected and completed His work of Redemption and Reconciliation on the Cross of Calvary, He suffered tremendously. He had nails driven through His hands and feet. He was beaten with a cord that had metals at the end of it that ripped through His flesh.

He even wore a crown of thorns that pierced His head. He suffered shameful taunting from the religious people and others of that time. His sufferings were unimaginable. My point is, He suffered. But then, He was given the authority of the chains of darkness and the keys of the bottomless pit. Finally, He became the first-fruits of the resurrection and inherited the glory of being the <u>Only One worthy of opening the seals in Revelation</u>. Jesus Christ suffered that we might live. Before He enjoyed the glory, He endured the sufferings.

Boaz took the risk and full responsibility that the first redeemer failed to take on. In the same way, Adam failed to carry out the divine mandate of leadership in his home. He did not cover his wife properly. He allowed her, as the "weaker vessel," to communicate with the enemy. That poor decision by Adam caused him to lose his power and rights of leadership. May I exhort all men, you have a God-given responsibility and divine power to be the spiritual leader of your home. It is your privilege to protect and provide for your home at all times. Men, please do not exercise weakness, but be a worthwhile leader in your home. The parallel between Adam and the first redeemer is very clear. Neither of the two wanted to take the risk that is involved in leadership. They wanted the easy way out. Many today are taking the easy way out, the path of least resistance. God is looking for men and women with strong and sturdy backbones, a spine that would not bend or break under pressure.

No one wants to suffer in this world. We are living in desperate and degrading times. These are the days of loose and wild living. People are compromising their faith to accommodate the standards of the world. You are hearing things like, "you can't hurt people's feelings," "you cannot be too hard on their lifestyles, after all, this is the trend." But let me remind you, <u>it took the precious blood of Jesus Christ that was shed on the Cross. None of us can ever imagine what it took for Him to endure it. None of us could ever imagine what pain and hurt it took the Father to turn His back on His Son because God could not look at the disease of sin that was upon His Son</u>. So, please do not try to tell me to take it easy on folks who are committing the awful acts of sin. Do not tell me to be careful what I say because I may hurt someone's feelings. My point is very clear. As Christians, you will suffer in this degrading world. You will be persecuted for the things of God, the real things that matter. Take heart and be hopeful. The suffering will end someday soon and you will enjoy the glory that He has prepared for you. There are tens of millions and maybe hundreds of millions of Christians around the world serving Christ. This is the result of the terrible sufferings that our Lord went through to accomplish. Our Jesus is enjoying this in glory and the devil is crying out in hell. Let us continue to do great exploits for the Lord and lead as many people to the Cross of Jesus Christ! As Boaz executed the power of attorney on behalf of Ruth, she enjoyed his gifts and goodness. In the same way, our Lord Jesus executed the power of attorney so that all born-again believers can enjoy all the gifts and goodness from above.

CHAPTER SEVENTEEN
RUTH ENJOYS THE PROMOTION

> *A promotion comes with many benefits. Similarly, believers in Christ are enriched with His goodness and empowered with His presence!*

Everyone at some time or the other enjoys promotions. I reflect the wonderful days at school during my childhood and young adolescent years. At the end of the school year, after writing exams in all the various subjects that were taught, I was given a report card to take home to my parents. I was thrilled with excitement and joy, not only from reading the wonderful results I got from the exams, but the one thing that topped it off was the notation at the bottom of the report card that read, "you have been promoted to the next Grade level." That brought a joy that was inexpressible and an elation that I could not explain. The reason was because my parents were extremely happy. Also, those who were concerned over my achievement were thrilled to the highest level. Similarly for Ruth, this promotion was beyond her expectation. As for the ones who witnessed that fabulous occasion, they were overjoyed and thrilled. Not only at school is one filled with emotion, but also on the job. When your boss said, "You have been doing a great job and your work was exceptional. I am proud to announce that you have been promoted to the manager's position!" What a great time of celebration! What am I talking about? When a promotion is given, you are definitely overjoyed because there are lots of benefits that come along with the promotion.

I remember when I started as a young preacher in 1978, in my home country of Guyana, SA. I received my District Minister's License to preach in that District. It made me feel very special and blessed. Why? Because I was not restricted to preach in a local church only, but I could have gone and preached throughout the entire district. I am not saying this out of a prideful heart because when God promotes you, humility is the key factor, however that does not mean you should not enjoy the promotion. I can go on and on with my promotions time after time. From District Minister's license to an Assistant Pastor and then fully to the position of Pastor. The promotions then went on, as I held different offices in the church, and finally the big promotion came when I was ordained to the Ministry as an elder and the District voted me as their Superintendent for all the Churches in Guyana. The offices varied in responsibilities but they were also enjoyable especially when I had to represent the church both nationally and internationally. That job had to be endured in the various challenges that were presented, but it was also enjoyable when placed in the hands of God.

Now I have to retract and get back to set in place how Ruth enjoyed the promotion. *"Then the elders and all those at the gate said, 'We are witnesses. May the Lord make the woman who is coming into your home like Rachel and Leah, who together built up the house of Israel. May you have standing in Ephrathah and be famous in Bethlehem.'"* Ruth 4:11. Ruth was recognized among some of the most influential and important matriarchs in Israel. Leah was responsible for bringing forth in this world six of the tribes of Israel and among them was Judah who was the predecessor of Jesus Christ. Rachel brought forth two tribes and one of them was Joseph who is actually a type of Jesus. So, to be named among the "greats" of Israel was a very special touch of class and a promotion worth talking about. That must have been a very touching moment for Ruth and "one of a kind." That endowment of special recognition came from the mouth of the elders of the leaders of Bethlehem. The men standing at the gate would be the most prominent of men. They were "no ordinary boys," so to speak, they were like the President of the United States Cabinet members, the ones who give the President the best advice and help him make the most strategic decisions. Those prominent men knew exactly what they did and what they said. The remarkable statement made by those men of importance might have taken Ruth by surprise. She probably thought that it was no ordinary compliment to be categorized with Leah and Rachel. However, she had Boaz on her side and that was what mattered the most. "*I can do everything through Him who gives me strength.*" Philippians 4:13.

The difference between you and the people of the world is the fact that you "*know whom you have believed in and you are persuaded that He is able to keep you,*" (II Timothy 1:12b) and accomplish whatever He so desires to accomplish through you. Ruth had the assurance that as long as Boaz was on her side, she would be successful. The calming effect of the Lord's presence in our lives and ministry is all we need to take us through this journey that may at times confront us with uncertainties and obstacles. The Lord's powerful and capable hand is not short as He leads us on, like He led Ruth through her journey.

There were two towns with the names Bethlehem. One was in Judah, the southern part of the Jewish homeland and the other Bethlehem was in the north. However, the Bethlehem in Judah, in the more ancient times is called Ephrathah. So, when the prophet Micah used the phrase, "Bethlehem Ephrathah," he was trying to make it clear that he was referring to a town of Bethlehem that used to be known as Ephrathah. In other words, this would be Bethlehem in Judah. I quote the following from a very famous Rabbi, David Kimchi, "Although thou art little among the thousands of Judah, out of thee shall come forth unto me a Judge to be ruler in Israel, and this is the king Messiah." David Kimchi has been a leading Hebrew grammar expert. Standard editions of the Hebrew Bible frequently included his learned and lucid commentaries. This information was cited from the website www. Infoplease.com using the keyword "kimchi". You might be asking the question why am I spending time explaining Ephrathah, Bethlehem. This was the place that Ruth was providentially led into as she became very popular because of the union between her and Boaz. This is not to be taken lightly but seriously and reverently. Ephrathah is also the same place that the Messiah was born. I believe we have to bring some clarity to the accuracy and genuine authority of the place. Not only Rabbi David Kimchi mentioned the fact of Bethlehem Judah, but if you read the Targum, Tanakh, reference was made about Ephrathah, also the Talmud, Berakoth 5a. From the inspired word of God in Genesis Chapter 35 and verse 16, mention is made of the place where Rachel was to give birth to her son Benjamin and then in verse 19 that place was mentioned again when she died.

Now fast forward to the prophet Micah. *"But you, Bethlehem Ephrathah, though you are small among the clans of Judah, out of you will come for me One who will be ruler over Israel, whose origins are from old, from ancient times."* Micah 5:2. The spiritual connection between Micah 5:2 and Ruth 4:11 is that it was the same place that was referred to the birth place of Jesus. Ruth, who was a young unknown girl, became the ancestress of our Lord and Savior, Jesus Christ. When God wants to use you for His honor and glory, it does not matter what nationality you are or what background you came from. What matters most is for you to be obedient to His call and to be ready to respond to Him in a positive way, like Ruth did.

Reflect with me for a moment on Ruth. Just a few years before, she had lost her husband and then her sister-in-law went back into idolatry. She could have given up as well because she heard many negative words from Naomi, her mother-in-law. Instead of receiving words of encouragement that would propel her forward, Ruth was bombarded with the wrong advice. And remember, she is now in the "House of Bread," which means Ruth should have only been surrounded with words of wisdom and encouragement. Does that sound familiar to you? Many people receive negative and repulsive words instead of receiving positive and uplifting words to move them forward in the Kingdom of God. You see, Ruth's life was steadfast and committed to Boaz so nothing negative or discouraging had any effect on her! When you are fully dedicated and committed to your Savior, you will have the same characteristics like Ruth. The words that came out of Ruth's mouth were, "where you go I will go, where you die I will die, your people will be my people, and your God will be my God." When Naomi heard such endearing words, she was amazed and could not have said anything further, but "alright let us go."

Ruth faced some spiritual turbulences along her spiritual path, but every time something ugly showed up, she was in the position to devour the enemy. Therefore, Ruth was ready to extend her legacy. Firstly, she did this by exercising patience during the process, and secondly, because Boaz executed the power of attorney. This bold step by Boaz came as a surprise for Ruth. Is that not what God does for us, surprises us along the way when we do not expect it to happen? She was steadfast and secure and that helped her to enjoy her promotion in Bethlehem. *"Does not the Scripture say that the Christ will come from David's family and from Bethlehem, the town where David lived?"* John 7:42. All of this became a reality because Ruth was not distracted, discouraged nor disengaged. She was enriched with the goodness of Boaz and empowered with his presence. Similarly, you who are believers in Christ can be enriched with His goodness and empowered with His presence!

CHAPTER EIGHTEEN
RUTH EMBODIED THE PROMISE OF THE REDEEMER

> *God will use whomever He wants in order for His will and purposes to be accomplished. Let the Holy Spirit open up your spiritual horizons where you can find your purpose in the Lord.*

This final chapter is the crowning episode of Ruth's amazing journey of faith. You will see how Ruth was used by God to become the ancestor of Jesus, our Savior. *"Through the offspring the Lord gives you by this woman, may your family be like that of Perez, whom Tamar bore to Judah. So Boaz took Ruth and she became his wife. Then he went to her, and the Lord enabled her to conceive, and she gave birth to a son."* Ruth 4:12-13. Who is Perez? Why is his name so significant to be mentioned among the echelons in Israel? Looking back, in the book of Genesis Chapter 38 and verse 6, it tells us that Judah's son, Er, was married to Tamar, but he was a very wicked man and the Lord put him to death. His brother Onan also died because he failed to bring forth seed for his brother, as was required at that time, according to Genesis Chapter 38 and verse 10. Judah had one younger son left by the name of Shelah and Judah promised to give him to Tamar when he grew up to be a man. But Judah never kept his promise, so Tamar disguised herself as a prostitute and enticed Judah to sleep with her. So what was the result of that act of fornication? Tamar brought forth twins and one of them was Perez. So, that is how Perez came into existence and played a very important role in the book of Ruth and also the genealogy of Jesus. After Perez was mentioned in the book of Genesis, interestingly, nothing was said about him again until in the book of Ruth.

Ruth and Boaz produced a son by the name of Obed. His name means, "servant" or "worshipper" in Hebrew. He became the grandfather of King David. Some commentators also thought Obed's name means, "encourager" which means he would encourage others to a higher calling. No doubt, Jesse was a true worshipper and so was his son, David. When we look back at Judah who committed fornication with Tamar and produced twin boys, we have to understand that the parents are the ones who did the wrong and not the children. Therefore, God will use whomever He wants in order for His will and purposes to be accomplished. Our God made it possible for all to be saved through the shedding of His Son's blood on the cruel cross of Calvary.

Now let me explain exactly how Ruth embodied the promise of the Redeemer. From the very inception of this wonderful story, Ruth showed and exemplified what it takes to be obedient to the Holy Spirit and also to work under the direction of the Holy Spirit. Not everyone can work under leadership and authority. For you to become a great leader, you must first master the art of being a good follower! This quality was found in Ruth. This is the reason why God chose her to be the pivotal contact in bridging the gap of the Redeemer. The gospel according to Matthew started the genealogy of Jesus from Abraham and ended with Christ (Matthew 1:1-16). But the Gospel according to Luke started the genealogy from the birth of Christ and went backwards to God directly (Luke 3:23-38). Ruth, a very pious person, became a very prominent and powerful woman in all of Israel. She became one of the greatest women of the Bible with enormous popularity and fame, even though her beginnings were small and insignificant. I want to exhort you, as you read this simple book that is filled with great possibilities, that you will allow the Holy Spirit to open up your spiritual horizons where you can find your purpose in the Lord. It is by no chance that you are reading this book even if it were given to you by a friend or maybe you have just stumbled over a copy. It is the direction of the Holy Spirit upon your life. I am pretty confident that as you draw closer to the conclusion of this book, God will bring to your mind revelations that you have not yet experienced. I pray for God's richest blessings to be poured out on your life, your family's, your ministry's, and your relationships. I also pray for God's favor and honor to surround you permanently. If you have been blessed, encouraged, challenged or uplifted in any way, please let me know because it will definitely be a blessing.

CONCLUSION

While some may want to call it a daring love story, (to which I have no problem), some may even say that it represents the atoning work of Christ, (which I certainly have no issues with), but when I began to gather the thoughts to write this book, my preference is, "The Marvelous Hand of God." The reason behind this title is simply how God took a young woman in the likeness of Ruth, brought her out of the land of Moab and into the beautiful land of Bethlehem. We saw several misfortunes during this amazing journey of Ruth. First, Elimelech made the decision to go to Moab because of the famine in Bethlehem. This famine in Bethlehem drove Naomi and her family to Moab to make a living for themselves. However, during their stay in Moab, Elemelech died and this brought pain to Naomi. If that were not enough, her two sons also died. The pain of the loss of her loved ones became so enormous that Naomi was not only devastated but depressed. During that process, her two boys were married to two Moabite women. So, not only Naomi grieved, but Ruth and Orpah also grieved their losses respectively. No one knew exactly what was going on except that God's plans and purposes were working out providentially. In all that tragedy, Ruth learned the secrets of trusting her redeemer to the fullest extent. Ruth was not bothered by the blistering that the enemy offered. Instead, her mind and heart moved in the direction that God wanted it to go.

You see, in our lives as well, there will be times when we get so blistered through the enemy's schemes and tricks, we will want to give up and turn back to the world. This is the time for you to focus on the cross of Jesus and find the hope and comfort like that which Ruth found. When you begin to see "God's Marvelous Hand" at work in your life, you will definitely experience all the blessings that the Lord has stored up for you. You will see His Divine favor and love in abundance bestowed

Dr Lawrence Chester

upon you. It is my sincere desire that after reading this book, you will fully experience His Marvelous Hand at work. This will be done when the Holy Spirit is in full control and operation.

For speaking engagements, please contact him by the following:
Pastor Lawrence Chester. Tel. 516-782-5324.
Email: larry.317@hotmail.com.

www.ingramcontent.com/pod-product-compliance
Lightning Source LLC
Chambersburg PA
CBHW071503070526
44578CB00001B/423